The Cathedral of Notre-Dame of Paris. A Quick Immersion

Quick Immersions provide illuminating introductions to diverse topics in the worlds of social science, the hard sciences, philosophy and the humanities. Written in clear and straightforward language by prestigious authors, the texts also offer valuable insights to readers seeking a deeper knowledge of those fields.

Kevin D. Murphy

THE CATHEDRAL OF NOTRE-DAME OF PARIS

A Quick Immersion

Tibidabo Publishing
New York

Published by Tibidabo Publishing, Inc. New York.

Copyediting by Jéssica Gómez
Cover art by Raimon Guirado
For illustration copyrights, please see page 7.

First published 2020

Visit our Series on our Web:
www.quickimmersions.com

ISBN: 978-1-949845-21-1
1 2 3 4 5 6 7 8 9 10

Library of Congress Control Number: 2020946204

Printed in the United States of America.

Contents

List of illustrations

Cover Illustration

Henri Matisse (1869-1954), View of Notre Dame.
Paris, Quai Saint-Michel, Spring 1914. Oil on canvas,
The Museum of Modern Art, New York, NY, USA.

Introduction

Chapter 2

Chapter 3

Chapter 4

Chapter 6

Chapter 7

Introduction

Notre-Dame: A Site of Memory

In the wake of the devastating fire at the Cathedral of Notre-Dame in Paris, French President Emmanuel Macron stated that the event "reminds us [the French people] that our history never stops." Indeed, the cathedral was not quite the perfect embodiment of the Gothic style that some commentators made it out to be, since its present form is the culmination of a building process that has lasted centuries, one that in fact is ongoing. Notre-Dame was largely constructed from 1163 to 1250 on or near the sites of a possible classical temple and four earlier Christian churches on the Île de la Cité, an island in the Seine River at the heart of Paris. However, Notre-Dame continued to evolve in subsequent times, undergoing periods of neglect or deliberate destruction that alternated with moments when resources were poured into the building's improvement or restoration. Indeed, the cathedral's current appearance largely derives from its restoration in the mid-nineteenth century, as did its much-lamented 750-ton spire that toppled in the fire of April 15, 2019.

In the days after the fire, I was contacted by a newspaper reporter who asked me whether Notre-Dame should be preserved and further, whether any building should be preserved. I found this question surprising since I assumed, apparently naively, that since both France and the United States have had vigorous historic preservation movements since the nineteenth century, as well as national government policies supporting the retention and repair of landmark buildings, it went without saying that most citizens believe that the historic built environment has value. My own research has focused on the process by which the two countries, independently for the most part, created public and private agencies to ensure that older buildings would be preserved in the face of cataclysmic change —particularly to historic construction and landscapes— brought about by the processes of industrialization and urbanization —of modernization more generally. With this history in mind, I responded to the reporter (astonished) that buildings —especially large and complex structures like Notre-Dame— represent the aspirations, ingenuity, and creativity of past generations. And in the case of premodern buildings, including the great churches and cathedrals of the Middle Ages, the fabric itself is our only tangible connection to the largely anonymous workers who actually constructed them. Out of respect for them and for their handiwork that now keeps the past present in the built environment, we should care for the buildings that are our legacy. Prosper Mérimée (1803-1870), a renowned French author and preservation advocate, made the point eloquently in 1846, in a published report to the Minister of the Interior. There, he acknowledged that business concerns preoccupied most people at that moment (not unlike today). "However," he asked rhetorically, "for a nation such as ours, the conservation of grand historical memories, the respect for works of art, are those not an obligation which we must never forget?"

For many of the vast numbers of people worldwide who watched with horror as Notre-Dame was engulfed in flame, it came as a surprise to learn that much of the fabric being consumed by fire was actually modern construction. They are not to be faulted for seeing the cathedral as a pure expression of the Middle Ages since the restoration of medieval buildings (and indeed, of buildings from all periods) has often emphasized their faultless correspondence to particular periods or styles. In France in the nineteenth century, and in the US in the twentieth, early preservationists preferred that restored buildings represent singular moments in the history of architecture rather than reflect the true nature of construction. In reality, even after buildings are considered "complete," they continue to grow or to diminish, to expand or shrink, in any case to change in response to the evolving needs of their owners, users, or both.

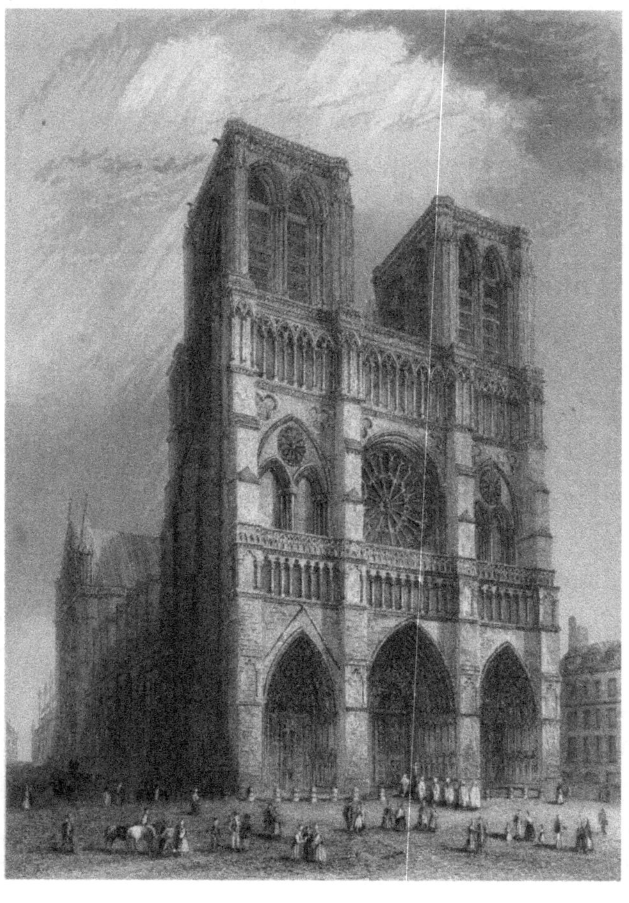

1. Notre-Dame Cathedral, West Front.

The authors of guidebooks probably believe it is too difficult for the lay reader to understand the complicated and often confusing processes by which the monuments of France, or of other countries, have achieved their current appearances. The French literary theorist, philosopher, cultural critic, and semiotician Roland Barthes noted as much in his volume *Mythologies* (1957) in a famous essay on the ubiquitous Hachette World Guides, or the *Blue Guide* as it is familiarly referred to. In his mind, the guidebook reduces the rich histories of European countries to simplistic displays of monuments devoid of any relationship to the process of change or to the real lives of people. He writes of the *Blue Guide*, "To select only monuments suppresses at one stroke the reality of the land and that of its people, it accounts for nothing of the present, that is, nothing historical, and as a consequence, the monuments themselves become undecipherable, therefore senseless." In a similar way, Notre-Dame, as many commentators demonstrated in 2019 when they insisted on the perfection of Notre-Dame as an embodiment of the Gothic style crafted during the Middle Ages, was not widely understood as an organic, living thing. Observers generally did not comprehend that the cathedral's original fabric had decayed and later been repaired, had been deliberately destroyed then restored, and in the process had registered in its very stones the many hundreds of years of French history it had witnessed. Authors of the 1856 monograph on the cathedral, the Baron

Ferdinand de Guilhermy (1809-1878) and Eugène-Emmanuel Viollet-le-Duc (1814-1879), had made a similar point when they asserted that "The history of Notre-Dame is connected in an intimate manner to the entire history of France." The two authors were part of the process later described by historian Pierre Nora whereby French monuments (and other objects and practices) become "lieux de mémoire," or sites of memory, where the nation's past is enshrined.

In the cycle of construction and destruction at Notre-Dame, the 2019 fire is undoubtedly the most cataclysmic event in the cathedral's history. Indeed, investigative reporting by the *New York Times* in July, 2019 showed "That Notre-Dame still stands is due solely to the enormous risks taken by firefighters in [the] third and fourth hours" following the discovery of the fire. One reason that the cathedral came so close to total destruction, argued the *Times*, was the confusion generated by the building's alarm system on April fifteenth, over where the fire was located, whether in the attic of the cathedral itself or of the adjacent sacristy. In reality, the fire was concentrated in the "forest," the original wood structural support system for the cathedral's main roof. That oak structure had protected the building below it since the time of its completion in the Middle Ages. An impressive engineering feat and a thing of great beauty in and of itself which is now completely lost, the wood roof structure had no fire suppression equipment or even fire barriers, the *Times* reported.

The Structure of Notre-Dame

Following the fire, one urgent task was to devise somehow a temporary covering for the building since that role was no longer being played by the roof. Exposed after April fifteenth were the stone vaults that sail above the nave, the main rectangular space of the cathedral that runs from the entry at the west to the altar and apse at the east. The term "vault" is defined by *Merriam-Webster's Dictionary* as "an arched structure of masonry usually forming a ceiling or roof." Gothic vaults are supported on the nave's exterior, and in the case of Notre-Dame, by the celebrated flying buttresses that extend over the aisles found at either side of the central section of the main sanctuary. These aisles allow for circulation around the nave and altar while mass is ongoing and are a common feature of pilgrimage churches from the medieval period. At that time, pilgrimage routes were established from Paris and other northern points to Santiago de Compostela in Spain as well as to Rome, the seat of the Catholic church. Pilgrims were attracted to churches and cathedrals along the pilgrimage routes by their relics, that is, to objects related to Jesus Christ, saints, or other figures sacred to Christians. As Cynthia Hahn writes in her book, *The Reliquary Effect: Enshrining the Sacred Object* (2016), "Through a framing action of physical context, legends and rituals, relics are identified and defined as *unique, authentic, powerful* and *effective*;"

encountering relics is believed to produce positive outcomes and they bring the holy figures closer for the faithful. An example is the Crown of Thorns believed to have been worn by Jesus before his crucifixion, which was housed Notre-Dame and was rescued from the cathedral as the fire was burning by Father Jean-Marc Fournier, chaplain of the Paris Fire Brigade.

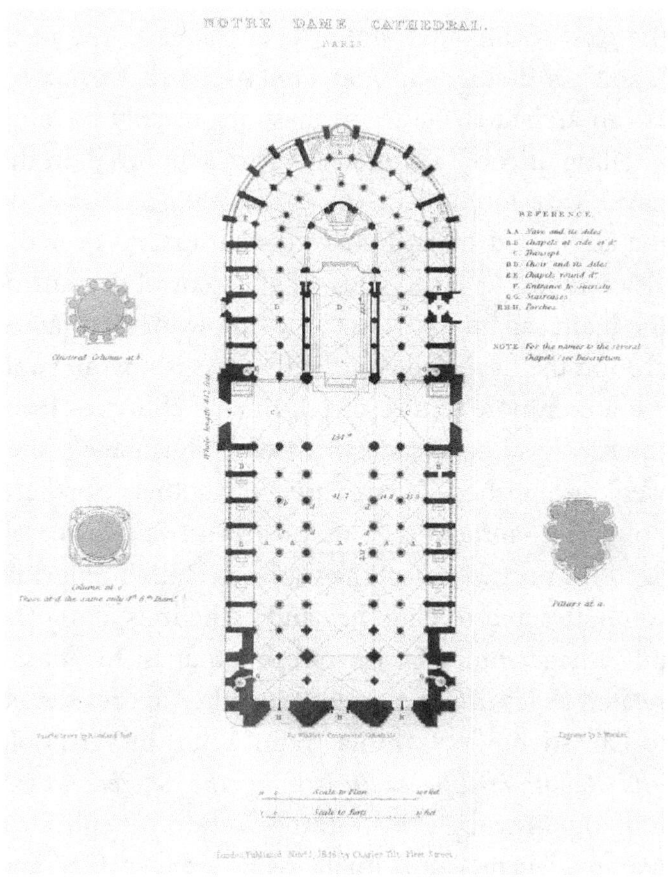

2. Notre-Dame de Paris, Plan.

The centuries-old wood structure of the forest quickly became an inferno after the fire started and engulfed the spire. The spire also had a wood structure, although of more recent vintage, and was covered with lead. When it fell, it took out sections of the vaults below. The fire also spread to the north facade tower where the wood structure within holds eight bells. It was feared that if the structure burned, then the bells would fall, taking the tower with them. The collapse of the north tower could have then brought down the south tower at the façade. Fortunately, the heroic efforts of Paris's firefighters saved both towers, and with them, the entire cathedral.

The April fifteenth fire brought worldwide attention to Notre-Dame de Paris and led many people to articulate their strong emotional connections to the building, the product variously of municipal or national pride, religious devotion, or passion for Gothic architecture. Years before the fire, art historian Michael Camille in his definitive study, *The Gargoyles of Notre-Dame, Medievalism and the Monsters of Modernity* (2009) beautifully articulated the significance of Notre-Dame when he described the cathedral as "the very face of France." Camille lauds Notre-Dame as an exceptionally innovative Gothic structure, but more important, he writes, "There are many churches dedicated to Notre Dame but only one Notre-Dame de Paris. Located on the east end of the Île-de-la-Cité, the cathedral is the spiritual and geographic center not only of Paris, but of the whole of France."

In the following seven chapters and postscript I lay out the process by which Notre-Dame achieved its status as a canonical medieval building, a representative of the Gothic style, and a symbol of Paris and the French nation. As I will show, that progression was neither straightforward nor inevitable; there were many points at which other stylistic preferences —notably, for classical architecture— worked against an appreciation of the Gothic and brought about a loss of historic fabric at Notre-Dame. The changing fortunes of the Catholic church, particularly during the period of the French Revolution, also spelled the destruction of some of the cathedral's original features. As the Rev. Dr. Scadding wrote of Notre-Dame in the *Toronto Maple Leaf* in 1848, "Time has stripped it of some of its attractions —and the destructive grasp of man has robbed it of even more. Many of the statues, pictures, and other costly decorations with which it was lavishly enriched by princes, ecclesiastics and corporations, shared the fate of other noble works of art in the excesses of the Parisian mob at the close of the last [eighteenth] century."

In describing the building's evolution, however, I avoid demonizing classicists or revolutionaries and instead focus on the contributions each period made to the building, even where it spelled the replacement of medieval parts with classical or modern elements. I want to show that Notre-Dame Cathedral has been a touchstone for Parisians for centuries, a resonant symbol of the faith for Christians everywhere, and an emblem of Frenchness for the French themselves, and for their allies, throughout the nation's history.

Organization of the Chapters

Chapter 1, "The Île de la Cité before Notre-Dame" situates Notre-Dame geographically and historically. This chapter positions the Île de la Cité within the city of Paris, from its ancient origins through the Middle Ages. For those unfamiliar with Paris and its early history, the chapter shows just where the cathedral stands in relation to the first settlements on the banks of the Seine. The chapter also briefly discusses the churches that stood on the site prior to the Gothic cathedral.

In Chapter 2, "The Gothic and Notre-Dame," I provide a brief overview of Gothic architecture as it is now believed to have developed. Its structural aspects, as well as its development out of the earlier Romanesque style, are addressed. This is where the construction history of Notre-Dame, as it is now understood, is laid out and where Notre-Dame is placed in the historiography of the Gothic.

Its cathedral occupies a particularly significant position in Paris, but Notre-Dame is only one —albeit the most recognized— of several Gothic buildings in the city. Nearby are the Sainte-Chapelle and the Church of Saint-Séverin, both Gothic —of the Rayonnant and Flamboyant strains respectively— and the late Gothic Church of Saint-Eustache is not far away. By comparing Notre-Dame to these and other Gothic monuments in Paris, Chapter 3 —"Gothic Paris"— clarifies its special architectural character.

The cathedral was never outside of politics, but Chapter 4, "Notre-Dame and Political Revolution" focuses on some of the most famous episodes in its history, those that changed its appearance and setting in fundamental ways. Famously, the Gallery of Kings on the façade of Notre-Dame was bashed during the French Revolution for the reason that its sculpted figures were believed to represent the despised —and deposed— monarchy. But that is only one time when Notre-Dame was at the center of political struggle. In 1830 and 1831, for example, the Palace of the Archbishop, which stood between the cathedral and the Seine, was deliberately destroyed. This chapter shows how the building's symbolic association with the church and monarchy led to its being embroiled in political controversies in the nineteenth and twentieth centuries.

The Emperor Napoleon's coronation marked the cathedral's cooptation for his political purposes. Moreover, because he was an ardent classicist, Napoleon supported alterations to Notre-Dame that worked against its medievalism by masking it with classical elements. These changes to the cathedral, outlined in Chapter 5, "The Classicists' Notre-Dame," represent the building's new political alignment at the turn of the nineteenth century.

As I show in Chapter 6, "Notre-Dame and the Medieval School," the publication of Victor Hugo's novel *Notre-Dame de Paris* (1831) was just one indication of a new esteem for Gothic architecture in France and indeed worldwide during the mid-nineteenth century. It was followed by an ambitious restoration project led by the renowned architect and theorist Viollet-le-Duc and his collaborator, Jean-Baptiste Lassus (1807-1857), starting in the mid-1840s and continuing through the 1860s. This chapter demonstrates the lasting impact this restoration has had on the monument and its site. Not only did the cathedral get virtually reconstructed structurally at this point, it also regained some of the elements —like sculpture— that had been destroyed during the Revolution, as well as the gargoyles, chimeras, and the now lost spire. This was also the point at which the "parvis" (or "square") was opened up at the west side of the building, a promenade created between the cathedral and the Seine, and a garden planted around the apse at the east.

A venerated historic monument, Notre-Dame has not stopped inspiring modern artists and architects, as Chapter 7, "The Modern Notre-Dame," shows. Although the nineteenth-century restoration had made Notre-Dame into a recognized image of the Gothic past, it nonetheless offered some direction to the development of modernism in art and architecture. Finally, the postscript brings the discussion up to date by referring to proposals for restoring the cathedral and possibly designing a new spire in a modern spirit. The global interest in the future of Notre-Dame has been phenomenal, as reflected in extensive coverage of the many rebuilding proposals, especially for its iconic spire.

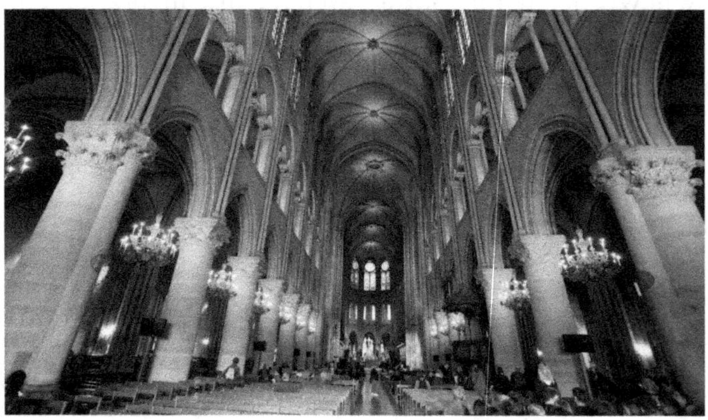

3. Notre-Dame de Paris, Nave.

Referring to this discussion, architect Garrett Nelli comments that, "This very may well be the first moment in human history where millions will have the opportunity to openly debate the value of the built environment in our lives." Maybe this is an overstatement. After all, the near complete destruction of the Gothic cathedral of Reims during World War I, and the total obliteration of the World Trade Center towers in New York City on 9/11, both occasioned debates about rebuilding that were avidly followed by international audiences. Nonetheless, the point remains: as much as the fire at Notre-Dame is unquestionably a disaster, it can also lead us to affirm the important place of historic buildings in our lives, and to confirm the significance of architecture to our senses of community.

Chapter 1
The Île de la Cité before Notre-Dame

Roman Paris

On the map of the Île de la Cité published in Jacques Antoine Dulaure's *Histoire physique, civile et morale de Paris depuis les premiers temps historiques jusqu'à nos jours* (1825-28) the present location of Notre-Dame is labeled "Antiquités," with no further detail about the site as it existed during the period of Roman domination of the city, during the first century BCE. That one word —"Antiquities"— is the tantalizing suggestion of what Dulaure believed to lie beneath the surface of Notre-Dame and to date back to the city's Roman origins. However impressive the medieval monument was, the invisible —yet intriguing— earlier history of the site had been debated at least since the eighteenth century. In 1710, blocks of stone were unearthed from beneath the cathedral's chancel and were found to belong to the "Pilier des nautes," a monument dedicated by the boatmen of Paris to the Roman Emperor Tiberius. Just to the east of the cathedral Dulaure located the Altar to Jupiter ("Autel à Jupiter"), referring to a first-century CE altar dedicated to Tiberius and Jupiter, thought to have been discovered in 1711. Elsewhere on the island, Dulaure identifies a prison, a fortress, a marketplace, and an antique funerary monument —all dating from the period in which the Romans were establishing an urban center on the present site of Paris.

Dulaure's suppositions were based on then-current archaeological knowledge; the 2002 exhibition held in the crypt at Notre-Dame —"Le Parvis de Notre-Dame, archéologie et histoire"— refuted many of these assumptions, the catalogue commenting that: "[...] contrary to what is frequently claimed, none of the monuments from the early Roman Empire that form part of the classical trappings of *urbanitas* are to be found on the Île de la Cité." The curators disputed the existence of a "governor's palace" during the Roman period on the east end of the island, as well as of the Temple of Jupiter, in both cases citing a lack of archaeological evidence for them. However much modern archaeology may have dispelled many of the myths surrounding the island's Roman past, it has not detracted from the fascination of its early history. As Marcel Poëte observed in 1908 (in his book *L'Enfance de Paris*), "It is useful to study the precise form [of the Île de la Cité], and follow step by step the evolution which from the formless Gallic city, sheltered on a little island, emerged to become the immense city which we admire, and from the humble settlement of the Celtic ages, [was born] one of the greatest representations of human progress that has ever existed." Indeed, the relatively modest origins of modern Paris —the world-class city— are obscure, yet they remain a focus of urban research.

Some important material remains that were found on the "essentially residential" Île de la Cité provide evidence of the Roman annexation of Transalpine Gaul in 122 BCE. This conquest was part of the larger expansion of the Empire through which the Mediterranean Sea came to be considered a "Roman lake" surrounded by territory under imperial control.

Nineteenth-century archaeologist Théodore Vacquer (1824-1899) did not concur with Dulaure's conclusions about the Roman presence in Paris, as historian Colin Jones has pointed out. Vacquer took advantage of the extensive excavations in Paris that resulted from the wholesale reconstruction of the city's fabric between 1853 and 1870 by the Baron Georges-Eugène Haussmann (1809-1891), Prefect of the Department of the Seine under the regime of Emperor Napoléon III, to investigate the material evidence of antiquity.

Vacquer later recalled that "I saw that every day and in all neighborhoods the navvy's spade was laying bare and destroying ancient sites." All of that digging —carried out in the course of "modernizing" the city— revealed the remnants of Roman buildings and structures that had not been seen in centuries.

The Parisii

On the Île de la Cité the Romans built on top of an earlier, destroyed Gallic settlement. In 53 BCE, Roman dictator Julius Caesar (100-44 BCE) wrote in Book Seven of his history of the *Gallic Wars* about "Lutetia (which is a town of the Parisii, situated on an island on the river Seine)" (7:58). And it was there, in 53 BCE, that he held a council of all the Gallic tribes (6:3), of which the Parisii were one, "on the eve of the Vercingetorix's rebellion" against the Romans. The name "Paris" derives from these early inhabitants of the area. As historians Philippe Velay, Brigitte Fischer, Dominique Morel and Bailey Young observed in the magazine *Archaeology* (Vol. 38, no. 6) in 1985, "The Gallic peoples of Paris, the Parisii defeated by Caesar in 52 BCE, were already city dwellers with a well-developed network of commercial trade routes along the rivers and a much-respected currency based on gold." Moreover, they occupied a crucial geographic and cultural position between two dominant groups: "[T]he Parisii belonged to each of the two cultural spheres more or less separated by the Seine —Gaul on the one hand, Rome on the other. From their island center in the midst of this river valley, the merchants and boatmen of the settlement, soon to be known as Lutetia, acted as brokers between these two different worlds."

The island settlement the Romans constructed on the Île de la Cité was one of three proximate centers, of which the other two were on the "Left" (south) and "Right" (north) banks of the Seine River respectively. The Left Bank center was developed with what the scholar of ancient infrastructure, Cornelis van Tilburg calls "the typical Graeco-Roman chess board grid with right-angled corners and parallel-running streets," found in Roman settlements; on the Right Bank were suburban areas. The residential Île de la Cité was not gridded in the same way. By the second century CE, public monuments were constructed in the Left Bank settlement, including an amphitheater, a forum, and baths. The latter were known before the nineteenth century, although sometimes misidentified as the fourth-century CE "palace" of the Emperor Julian. Jones credits archaeologist Vacquer with having "identified for the first time the late Antique rampart on the Île de la Cité, the Roman street plan, a theatre on the Rue Racine, a forum and associated buildings on the Rue Soufflot, cemeteries out beyond the Luxembourg gardens and in the south-east of the city close to the Gobelins, and an amphitheatre by the Rue Monge" (*Transactions of the*

Royal Historical Society, Vol. 17 [Dec., 2007]: 157-83). Fragments of the Roman baths of Paris found on the Left Bank are now incorporated into the Musée de Cluny. The Mount of Sainte-Geneviève, also on the Left Bank, was the Capitol of Lutetia. The city's important buildings were the familiar monumental components of a Roman city: they were found in the imperial capital itself as well as in more far-flung settlements. More such buildings survive in other French cities which, although dwarfed by Paris today, were much larger in Roman times —Nîmes and Arles among them.

While the Romans developed their urban settlement on either side of the Seine, "the original center chosen by the conquered Gauls still remained the Île de la Cité," observed Charles Picard. It was "a vital nucleus, a periodic meeting-place for markets and doubtless also for pilgrimages." Under the Romans, the Île de la Cité was in the path of the "cardo maximus," the principal north-south road that connected the parts of any Roman city or encampment. Archaeological investigations reveal that a bridge was constructed across the Seine about fifty years following the Roman conquest of Lutetia.

Two centuries after the establishment of the Roman city, the Roman Prince and eventual Emperor Julian (331/32 CE-363 CE), who was in Gaul from 355 to 361 CE, recalled in writing his "beloved Lutetia —for that is how the Celts call the capital of the Parisii." "It is a small island lying in the river;" he wrote, "a wall entirely surrounds it, and wooden bridges lead to it on both sides." The reliability of the Seine was a plus for the settlement in Julian's estimation: "The river seldom rises and falls, but usually is the same depth in the winter as in the summer season." The omnipresence of river water had its impact on the local hydrology which was reflected in the place's name, as Jones suggests: "The city had originally been located on a marshy bog in a meander of the river Seine —the name Lutetia probably derived from *lutum*, Latin for mud or muck." It will surprise the modern reader to hear Julian add of the Seine that "it provides water which is very clear to the eye and very pleasant for one who wishes to drink." Julian also praised the mild Parisian climate which made possible the cultivation of grapes, "and some persons have even managed to make fig-trees grow by covering them in winter with a sort of garment of wheat straw and with things of that sort [...]" (Julianus Augustus, *Misopogon*, 340-341).

The wall around Lutetia, which Julian mentions, dated to the period after 275 CE when Franks, Alani, and other barbarians devastated Roman settlements located in an area that stretched from the Alps at the northeast to the Pyrenees in the southwest. In 1950 (in *Archaeology* 3:2 [June, 1950]: 112-118), historian Charles Picard dramatically described the impact of the invasion on the Île de la Cité and on the architectural projects of the Romans: "Then mutilated Paris had to retreat to the Île and there shut itself up as if besieged. The enclosure reconstructed about the year 300 borrowed from the buildings of Roman Paris, the tiers of the amphitheater, etc., everything in the rubble of civilization that could prove useful." More recent research dates the fortifications to between 308 and 360. As a result of the reuse of materials from earlier monuments for the fortifications around the Île de la Cité, very little of the ambitious building projects of the Romans survived. Paris, however, did continue as a settlement after Julian was declared Emperor in 361 and after "Valentinian I installed himself, in a residence [the palace] whose comfort had been praised by Julian." From Paris, the Romans continued to defend navigation on the Seine.

Merovingian Paris

Nonetheless, the Frankish King Clovis led a successful invasion of the city and established Paris as the capital of his new kingdom. The Merovingian kings, "the first post-Roman rulers of what now makes up much of France, Belgium, and Germany" (as historian John J. Contreni succinctly describes them in *French Historical Studies*, Vol. 19, No. 3 [Spring, 1996]: 755-756) have sometimes been caricatured as "do-nothing kings." In fact, however, they established a cultural foundation for the "renaissance" that occurred during the Carolingian empire that followed them. Converted to Christianity by 508 CE, Clovis constructed churches to serve the religion and set in motion the establishment of Paris as an important Christian center, a development that eventually led to the construction of Notre-Dame centuries later.

Clovis's church-building program went well beyond the Île de la Cité, the Merovingian's fortified stronghold, as archaeological excavations have demonstrated. Such investigation has been limited, as preservationist Catherine Brut points out in her contribution to the important collection of essays *Autour de Notre-Dame* (2003), by the fact that some Merovingian church remains are contained within later churches where digging is impractical and by the sheer lack of excavation. Many Merovingian churches are known only through references in historical documents, surviving sarcophagi, or architectural fragments. The most splendid of the Merovingian churches certainly stood on the Île de la Cité.

The ramparts of the island plainly supported the construction of the first Christian basilica there, dedicated to St.-Étienne (St. Stephen) located to the west of the current cathedral, under the towers and *parvis*. The first evidence of the church was revealed by Vacquer in 1847 while later excavations of the *parvis*, carried out under the direction of archaeologist Michel Fleury between 1965 and 1970, revealed that the south wall of St.-Étienne was constructed literally on top of the island's ramparts. Moreover, Fleury showed that the basilica was ambitious, from the perspectives of both sheer scale and architectural sophistication. On either side of its nave there were two aisles, which is remarkable enough as an indication of size, but the basilica's dimensions —100 feet wide and nearly 220 feet long— also suggest a very large building. The sophistication of the design, as Spencer P. M. Harrington reports (in *Archaeology*, Vol. 53, No. 2 [March/April 2000]: 52-57), was attested to by St.-Étienne's lavish materials and frank invocation of the major cathedral of Christendom: "[W]ith black and gray marble columns imported from the Pyrenees, [St.-Étienne] was the largest church of its time in Frankish Gaul and was modeled after the first basilica of St. Peters in Rome." Fleury's archival and archaeological research suggested that St.-Étienne was built during the reign of Merovingian King Childebert, between 511 and 558, and that the project was an expression of both his personal political ambition and his expansion of the Frankish empire. More recently, Alain Erlande-Brandenburg, an expert on Notre-Dame's history and architecture, has proposed that the church could predate the arrival of the Franks on the Île de la Cité and could have motivated their choice of Paris as a capital.

The extraordinary scale and beauty of St.-Étienne was recognized in its time by the Merovingian court poet Venatius Fortunatus (530-609) in his work, *De Ecclesia Parisiaca*. There he described the marble columns that supported the "resplendent nave" and the windows that with their glass diffused the sunlight entering the building and supported the poet's comparison of the cathedral with the Biblical Temple of Solomon.

Childebert's project established, to some degree, the cosmopolitanism of the Île de la Cité by invoking Old St. Peter's, the seat of the Catholic Church. That building had in turn adapted the basilica form, first developed by the Romans to suit a variety of purposes. The basilica was an architectural "type," distinguished by its rectangular plan with a semicircular apse, as well as its "high central nave and lower side aisles." Architectural historian Mark Gelertner observes that the basilica has provided "the essential organizing principle for ancient Roman law courts, Romanesque churches, Gothic cathedrals," and more modern buildings that fulfill a variety of functions. By using the basilica form, early Christians adopted a practical solution to creating a large space that suited ceremonial and ritual functions; they also expressed a cultural connection to the earlier practices of pagan Rome. When Childebert made reference at St.-Étienne to the basilica of Old St. Peter's he at once created a symbolic connection with the center of the Christian world and grounded his own imperial ambitions in those of the Roman leaders who had preceded him.

The Merovingians built a number of significant churches, many of them located in the Paris region. Among them was the church at St.-Denis, on the outskirts north of Paris, where, in the twelfth century, the Abbot Suger would famously construct what is generally regarded as the first Gothic church. However, as architectural historian William Clark has shown, Suger —like other medieval builders— incorporated earlier Merovingian elements into the rebuilt church. Gothic builders thereby established a visual connection with Merovingian architecture, which in turn visually reflected its reliance on Roman forms.

The Carolingian Dynasty, the Capetian Kings, and the Île de la Cité

The last Merovingian king, Childeric III, was deposed by Pepin the Short 751 who had himself crowned king and thereby established the Carolingian dynasty. Charlemagne, the most renowned Carolingian ruler whose name became synonymous with the dynasty, ruled as monarch from 768 to 800 and as emperor from 800 to 814, presiding over the Carolingian capital of Aachen (also known as Aix-la-Chapelle) where he encouraged what is often referred to as a "renaissance" of classical learning and culture. At that point, Paris served a diminished role in the empire while St.-Denis gained in significance. The Carolingian rulers who followed Charlemagne were not able to preserve the extensive empire he had assembled: they divided the territory he had controlled and the imperial line finally died out in 987 when Hugh Capet rose to power, establishing the Capetian kingship which would endure until 1328.

With the rise to power of the early Capetians, Paris became the center of the French kingship.

In Merovingian times, St.-Étienne was accompanied by two other basilicas on the Île de la Cité —one dedicated to the Virgin (Notre-Dame) and the other to St. Germain. Following the sack of Paris by the Normans in late December 856, Notre-Dame was rebuilt on a larger scale, according to historian Marcel Aubert, and adopted by the Bishop of Paris as his principal seat. A chapter of monks was established there in the eighth century and had a cloister located north of Notre-Dame. Thereafter Notre-Dame took on increasing importance and St.-Étienne declined in significance. By 1112-1116, concludes Aubert, St.-Étienne was already virtually in ruins, while Notre-Dame "reconstructed after the fire of 857, [was] restored and doubtless enlarged during the first years of the twelfth century" (*Comptes rendus des séances de l'Académie des Inscriptions et Belles-Lettres*, 1939). More recently, in his monograph on Notre-Dame (1998), Erlande-Brandenburg has proposed that the two dedications —to St. Stephen and to the Virgin— do not necessarily imply the existence of two somewhat separate buildings, but rather of one large structure divided into two parts by partitions: one (Notre-Dame) for the use of the canons and the other for the use of the bishop (St. Stephen).

The choir of the ninth-century Notre-Dame occupied the space now held by the first two bays of the current choir of Notre-Dame, and the older nave projected into the first bays of the cathedral's current nave. In other words, the earlier Notre-Dame was a smaller building which could be nested within the east end of the new and larger cathedral. Aubert argued that the apse of the old Notre-Dame remained in place up to the moment that the new choir was constructed, in 1163, and that the old nave stayed until it was replaced by the new one around 1180. From its origins then, Notre-Dame evolved incrementally as portions of the earlier building were demolished to make space for the new structure, section by section.

In the early medieval period, other religious buildings filled out the group on the Île de la Cité. To the north of St.-Étienne stood the baptistery of Saint-Jean le Rond (demolished in the eighteenth century) and the church of St.-Germain, referred to previously (demolished in 1802). To the east of the present cathedral, just beyond its apse, stood the church of Saint-Denis du Pas which was believed to have been erected on the spot where Saint Denis himself was martyred. In fact, synthesizing the architectural and archaeological research up to the time of her writing around 2003, Brut concluded that there were more than a dozen "edifices or religious establishments" constructed on the Île de la Cité before the middle of the twelfth century.

The activity generated by all of these religious buildings was complemented by what took place around the palace located at the western end of the island. It had been constructed by the Romans and occupied, as noted above, by Julian and later by Valentinian I. Monique Delon writes in her monograph on the Conciergerie (on the site of the earlier palace), that "From the Gallo-Roman period onwards, the Île de la Cité [was] divided into two centres. A spiritual centre to the east, where the temple was to be found and the cathedral would be built; a residential centre to the west, with the governor's palace, a robust fortress surrounded by ramparts." There, in 360, "Julian," the "apostate," "was declared emperor by his soldiers." Under the Merovingians the palace continued to be used, including by Clovis from 508 until his death there in 511. During the Carolingian period, when the capital was at Aachen, the building saw less use, although it was reoccupied, renovated, and expanded by the Capetians at the end of the tenth century to become the Palais de la Cité.

The Île de la Cité as developed by the Capetians was described by the writer Guy de Bazoches in 1175, just after the Gothic Notre-Dame we know today was begun, as the "the head, the heart, the very marrow of the whole city" (quoted by Colin Jones, *Paris: The Biography of a City*, 2006). The Capetians had established two faubourgs (or suburbs) on the Left and Right Banks, dedicated to teaching and learning, and to commerce respectively. These two centers were connected to the island by stone bridges —the "Grand Pont" extending to the Right Bank and the "Petit Pont" to the Left. From then on, the island with Notre-Dame as its most prominent landmark was the epicenter of Paris, and some would argue, of the nation, however much the building would remain a work in progress.

Chapter 2

The Gothic and Notre-Dame

Emergent Gothic

In his ambitious 1920 monograph on the Cathedral of Notre-Dame, Marcel Aubert stated his intention to write a comprehensive account of the building's history that synthesized all the previous scholarship. Further, he wrote that, "I want to specify one point in the history of Notre-Dame and show the place it occupies in the evolution of architecture, a moment at which Gothic art was born and flourished, from the middle of the twelfth century to the first years of the fourteenth. It was during this period that the monument was fashioned little by little, as we know it, while the work executed since that time has merely consisted of maintenance, often maladroit, or sometimes exaggerated restorations." While Aubert acknowledged the incremental process by which Notre-Dame had —"little by little"— come into being, he felt that the cathedral had achieved its ideal form in the late Middle Ages. Everything done to the building after that time he considered either botched maintenance work or overly aggressive restorations. While adhering to Aubert's conception of Notre-Dame as a building that only gradually emerged on the foundations of an earlier structure, I will depart from his point of view by thinking of the cathedral as a work that continued to change and evolve well after the fourteenth century. Still, it is important to situate Notre-Dame within the history of Gothic architecture, the principal goal of this chapter.

Aubert considered Notre-Dame to be "the last in a series of great churches that began with Saint-Denis and Anglo-Norman churches." In other words, he argued, Notre-Dame was built —figuratively— on the foundations of Suger's pioneering work at St.-Denis as well as on earlier Romanesque architecture. For Aubert, the consecration of the choir of St.-Denis on 11 June 1144, in the presence of monarchs, lords, five archbishops, and fourteen bishops, marked "the triumph of the Gothic style." More contemporary scholars, such as Christopher Wilson writing in his 1990 survey of *The Gothic Cathedral*, are more measured about the influence of English or French

Norman architecture on the development of the Gothic, but they continue to locate the origins of the style in the Abbey Church of St.-Denis —a key point of departure for Notre-Dame. Wilson also identifies a small group of churches that immediately preceded St.-Denis chronologically (in the 1130s) and were also located in the Île-de-France, the region around Paris in which "architects first achieved their paradoxical goal of combining high rib vaults with walls so thin as to be by themselves incapable of supporting such a heavy load."

Wilson echoes, to some degree, Viollet-le-Duc's nineteenth-century description of the central goal of the Gothic builder, which he considered to have been the creation of large, open interiors covered by stone vaults. Moreover, Viollet-le-Duc believed that medieval architects had also met the dual imperatives of making taller naves while simultaneously reducing the bulk of their walls, in part to open them up for expanses of stained glass, a feature that was indispensable to the Abbot Suger's concept of his church. There was no escaping the necessity of holding up the stone vaults even as the walls of Gothic buildings were reduced to glass-covered skeletons, so the structurally supportive role of the walls was consequently externalized to buttresses, which became increasingly elaborate through the mid-twelfth century. In the entry on "Construction" in his influential *Dictionnaire raisonné de l'architecture française du XIe au XVIe siècle* (1854-68) Viollet-le-

Duc confided that "The construction of vaults was thus the great preoccupation of the architects of the Middle Ages." To "minimize the effects of the thrusts of their vaults," medieval builders had used the lightest possible stone for them, argued Viollet-le-Duc, and "reduced thickness" of masonry as much as they could. They also adopted the pointed (or "broken") arch in place of the semicircular Romanesque arch to support nave vaults, while simultaneously creating systems of support outside the nave walls.

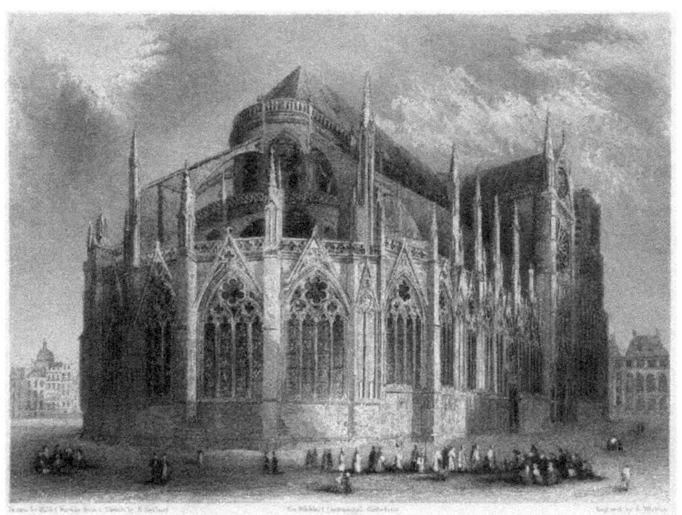

4. Notre Dame Cathedral, East End, showing flying buttresses.

Those systems were typically comprised of buttresses, which at Notre-Dame have the particularly spectacular form that is referred to as a "flying" buttress. Architectural historian William Clark describes how these elements work structurally: "A buttress consisting of two parts: the flyer arch, either segmental or quadrant, transmits thrusts from the vault and the high, exposed timber roof of a Gothic building across the aisle to the outer, upright support or buttress" (Grove Art Online). In other words, the upper, more horizontal portion of the buttress forms a kind of bridge between the vaults with the roofs above them, and the buttresses standing outside the exterior walls of the sanctuary. The "flyer" thus transfers the thrust of the vaults —no longer carried by the wall below which has been diminished in bulk by the insertion of stained glass— to the buttresses. While the flying buttress had been used since Roman times, it became a salient feature of French Gothic architecture by 1200, according to Clark. As we will see, understanding the contribution of Notre-Dame to the development of the flying buttress is a key issue for scholars of Gothic architecture.

The Gothic Schema

By the early twelfth century, suggests Wilson, "the normal scheme for a great church" had been established in northern France, outside the Île-de-France. It included "a Latin cross plan, a crossing tower, galleries, and a chevet with an ambulatory and radiating chapels". Thus, the essential form of the Gothic church or cathedral was built on a rectangular plan, ultimately derived from the

Roman basilica type, and ideally oriented with the apse at the east end and the entrance at the west. Intersecting the nave at a right angle, and thereby making the building's plan into the form of a cross, was the transept whose exterior facades were oriented to the north and south respectively. A tower typically marked the intersection —or "crossing"— of the nave and transept. At the east was the choir, the chevet (or "chevette") an ambulatory, a semicircular pathway, to facilitate the movement of pilgrims (in churches and cathedrals where they were numerous) from one side aisle to the opposite one, around the east end of the building, past chapels that radiated outward. This ideal plan provided a central space for a main altar and the celebration of the mass; it also facilitated the movement of lay people around the church or cathedral interior so that the clergy could perform their functions without interference.

The inclusion of galleries in the formula Wilson describes for the design of great churches is also significant for it suggests how the interior walls of the nave would be treated throughout the Gothic period. The term "gallery" refers to the story above the aisles at either side of the nave. The gallery runs above the first-story arcade which is comprised of piers that alternate with openings bridged by arches. Like the aisles below, the gallery is open to the nave. In large and complex buildings like Notre-Dame cathedral, it is just one of several components of the nave elevation, or wall, which could be (and was) treated in different ways over the course of time. In a three-story nave elevation, a clerestory above the gallery would provide windows looking out over the roofs of the aisles. In addition, a triforium was sometimes inserted (in a four-story elevation) below the clerestory and above the gallery; it was a passage no deeper than the wall, running above the gallery.

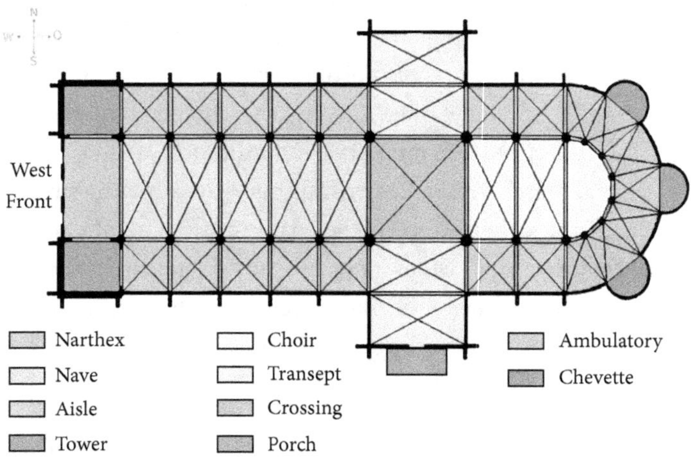

5. Floor plan of a basilica.

The Role of Abbot Suger

The transformation of this architectural formula into a model of the Gothic church or cathedral has generally been credited to the Abbot Suger; as Wilson observes, "Over the last hundred and fifty years it has become customary to begin histories of Gothic architecture with the choir added in 1140- 44 to the abbey church at St.-Denis, II km north of central Paris." Indeed, *A History and Description of the Royal Abbaye of Saint Denis* published in London in 1795 concluded that the building was "celebrated (independently of any religious sentiment) through all parts of Europe; and [was] an object of admiration to travellers, from every quarter of the globe." Perhaps this anonymous author overstated the tourist traffic to St.-Denis, but as Wilson concedes, its significance was not only architectural: the building was equally notable for its "splendour" and its connection to the monarchy. Typical of the appreciation shown the church over the centuries, our British visitor from 1795 praised St.-Denis's "riches," "superb decorations," "beautiful works of art," "treasures," and more. A decade or so later, other British authors —including James Dallaway in his *Observations on English Architecture* (1806) and George Downing Whittington in his book, *An Historical Survey of the Ecclesiastical Antiquities of France: With a View to Illustrate the Rise and Progress of Gothic Architecture in Europe* (1809)— identified St.-Denis as the first fully realized Gothic building. That status was confirmed by subsequent nineteenth-century antiquarians, both British and French.

The lavish appointments of St.-Denis were due to the patronage of King Louis VI who selected the monastery from among a number located on the outskirts of Paris as a place to store the royal crown and coronation regalia. St.-Denis was also a royal burial place and was associated with a saint who was credited with having defended the Christian faith in Gaul when he was sent to Paris from his native Italy by Pope Fabian. Despite persecution by the Roman authorities, Saint Denis was said to have persisted in his religious teaching, eventually becoming bishop, until his imprisonment (with two others) and their ultimate beheading around 250. According to legend, the miracle performed by the future Saint Denis was to carry his severed head from Paris —the site of his martyrdom— to the present location of St. Denis. Much to the benefit of the Benedictine monastery at St.Denis, the identity of this patron saint of France was later conflated with two others: Dionysius the Areopagite and the Pseudo-Dionysius, the composer of the Areopagitic writings. "But," wrote Joseph Stiglmayr in 1908 (in *The Catholic Encyclopedia*), "it was only through the 'Areopagitica' written in 836 by Hilduin, Abbot of Saint-Denis, at the request of Louis the Pious, that this serious error took deep root." This case of mistaken identity —the conflation of Saint Denis with the two Dionysiuses— enhanced the royal attraction to and investment in St.-Denis.

The Abbot Suger (c. 1081-1151) came from a "humble background" according to many of his biographies, but he rose in status to become a confidant of both Louis VI and Louis VII; he eventually served as the regent of France during the Second Crusade (in 1147) —his social and political position was that high. Suger had met Louis VI at

St.-Denis in his boyhood when the two were students there. As King, Louis VI entrusted Suger with some diplomatic missions prior to his appointment as abbot of St.-Denis in 1122. In that capacity, Suger reformed the monastery and rebuilt the church itself —in a very creative and influential manner. Suger's architectural and administrative intentions are well known because of the written record he left of his work: *Liber de rebus in administration sua gestis* (*Book on the Things Accomplished during his Administration*). There, Suger recorded the inscription on the doors to the church he rebuilt: "The noble work is bright, but being nobly bright it should brighten the mind, allowing it to travel from [earthly] light to the true light, where Christ is the true door." This brief passage embodies the "anagogical" principle of light, which maintained that a faithful Christian could ascend spiritually towards God through the contemplation of light. Suger's innovation —or one of them— at St.-Denis, was to make that light visible, by including as much stained glass as possible in the walls of the church which transformed the light as it passed through areas of pigment into brilliant colors visible to the eye. Maximizing the amount of light in the church required minimizing the amount of wall, and to bring about that transformation in the 1130s and 1140s, Suger extended the architectural innovations seen elsewhere in the Île-de-France with respect to the production of vaulted spaces.

Gothic St.-Denis

The reconstruction of the Carolingian church of St.-Denis under Suger began at the west end, with the main entrance. Suger demolished the first two bays, or sections, of the west end of the church and reconstructed the façade to create three portals —recalling the form of a Roman triumphal arch— with the central doorway being the largest and most important. Above it, at the upper level of the façade was installed a circular, or "rose" window, of stained glass, and finally, the elevation culminated in two towers (of which one survives). Paul Frankl, in his 1962 volume *Gothic Architecture* (later revised by Paul Crossley) argues that although the elements of the west elevation of St.-Denis were found in earlier Romanesque facades —including the triple doorways, circular windows, and pairs of towers— "In Saint-Denis," however, "the style is no longer Romanesque. This is not just a matter of the appearance of a few pointed arches —in the two flanking doorways, and in the blind arcades and glazed windows— nor the force of the projecting buttresses and their predominantly vertical emphasis." As important as pointed arches and buttresses are in Gothic buildings, there is also a unified and sculptural treatment of the parts of the façade that makes St.-Denis truly different from its predecessors. In addition, Suger's unnamed architect called for battlements at the top of the façade, an element that recalled defensive buildings like castles.

Wilson considered these features, together with elements borrowed from earlier royal churches and the prominent use of sculpture, to "leave no doubt that Suger intended the new entrance to embody a multiplicity of regal associations both earthly and celestial."

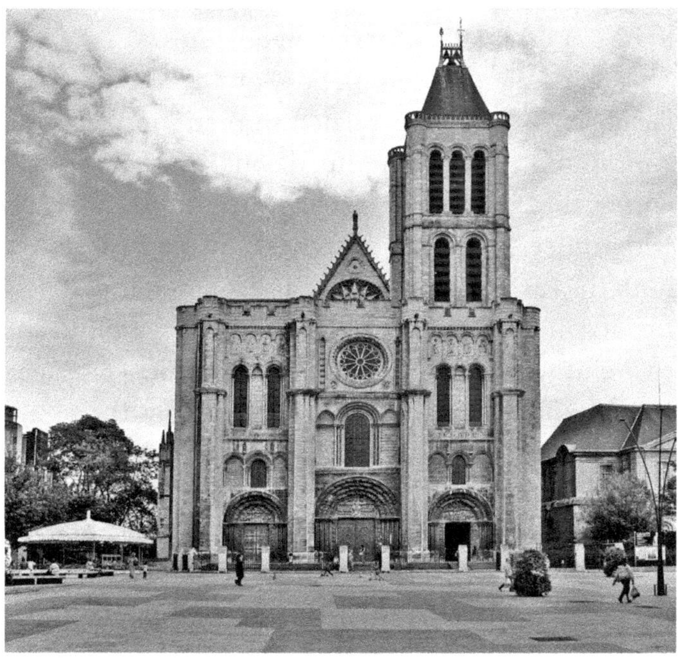

6. Façade of the Basilica of Saint-Denis.

Another indication of a new architectural approach observable at St.-Denis is the extent of sculpture, especially at the façade. Romanesque churches and cathedrals had certainly possessed sculpture and it played a crucial role in conveying to the faithful the teachings of the church and more.

There was no tradition of sculptural production in the Île-de-France at the time so Suger had to import sculptors from elsewhere. At the portals, full-size sculpted figures (now lost) were integrated into the colonettes in the jambs —the deep recesses that frame the doors. In later Gothic churches and cathedrals, including at Notre-Dame, the portals would continue to be important sites for sculpted figures.

Following the completion of the rebuilt west façade in 1140, Suger turned to rectifying what he considered to be the cramped conditions of the east end of the church, particularly around the altar. As with other medieval churches and cathedrals, in both the earlier Romanesque and later Gothic styles, the accommodation of pilgrims moving around the east end was a paramount concern at St.-Denis. As Frankl and Crossley write, "Presumably the abbot and his architect decided together not to have only one ambulatory with seven chapels around the main apse, but to dispense with the wall separating the chapels, and in this way create a second ambulatory round the first." The spatial effect was novel and contrasted sharply with the earlier west end of the church: while the construction of the two west bays was heavy, in part to support the towers, the east end was light. Moreover, the use of stained glass transformed the sunlight that entered the ambulatory, suffusing it with color.

The ambulatory vaults are supported by single columns in contrast to the compound piers which had been developed in other monumental religious buildings in the Île-de-France. Wilson contrasts the support for the choir at St.-Denis, which is provided by single —tho' substantial— columns, with other medieval interiors where analogous structural elements took the appearance of colonettes (or small columns) bundled together in a variety of ways, effectively masking the massiveness of the piers that they constituted. In other words, where the architect of the St.-Denis choir used single, large columns to hold up the vaults, earlier Gothic designers had used massive piers that were formed by groups of smaller columns attached to one another. The substitution of columns at St.-Denis for such compound piers created a structural challenge for its builders and led to "a radically new version of the 'skeletal' structure" (Wilson). The capitals that surmount these columns were also innovative and represented a shift away from how such elements were treated in earlier, Romanesque churches and cathedrals. While Romanesque church interiors are famous for their sculpted column capitals illustrating religious themes —often in emotionally charged, gripping detail— those at St.-Denis are based on leafy forms.

Wilson argues that the radical new concept of church design advanced at St.-Denis did not evolve rapidly into what has sometimes been called the mature, "High" Gothic style; rather, he suggests that novel ideas embodied in the choir of St.-Denis "were explored at a fairly leisurely pace and with comparatively few surprising consequences." Begun around 1160, the choir of Notre-Dame was part of this "leisurely" adoption of the innovations seen at St.-Denis.

The Gothic Style at Notre-Dame

The early Gothic architectural style that emerged at St.-Denis and was continued in other buildings in the Île-de-France and beyond, was considered "modern" at the time —as paradoxical as that mean seem to us. At the same time, woven into the new mode were ancient elements like the classicizing columns in the St.-Denis choir that reappear at Notre-Dame. Even more, the novel concept of the church or cathedral as a light-filled vessel whose walls are relatively thin and skeletal to support ribbed vaults lifted high above the viewer, also found its expression in Paris's cathedral.

At once startlingly new and steeped in the past, the first Gothic architecture combined a sense of obeisance to the buildings of earlier times and openness to exploring new forms and exploiting novel structural possibilities. As we have seen, at Notre-Dame the Gothic structure emerged gradually from the earlier building on the site and now we are in a position to appreciate how its design arose from the cutting-edge concepts that Suger brought into being at St.-Denis.

Building Phases at Notre-Dame

The realization of Notre-Dame resulted from the visions of several patrons and architects, not to mention the labor of many generations of workers, craftspeople, and artists. The process of design and construction has been usefully broken down into phases by the architectural historian Alain Erlande-Brandenburg in his definitive study, *Notre-Dame de Paris* (1998) —he cannot seem to lavish enough praise on the "harmonious," "beautiful," and "serene" building. As has already been noted, the cathedral of Notre-Dame was renovated and expanded in the early twelfth century, but soon after the Archdeacon of Paris, Maurice de Sully (d. 1196) was made bishop in October, 1160, he embarked on a dramatic and ambitious rebuilding of his cathedral. Over more than three decades, de Sully realized a part of his vision for the building, with the assistance of two different architects whose identities are unknown. The work was continued by two subsequent designers in the early thirteenth century, and, as Erlande-Brandenburg writes, "During the 1250s, Jean de Chelles was charged with designing the new transept; he completed its northern arm but not its southern one, which was completed after his death in 1258 by his successor, Pierre de Montreuil." (The transepts reflected the twin dedications of the earlier cathedral and church on the site: the northern one to the Virgin and the southern one to St. Stephen.)

Another architect was responsible for adding the chapels of the chevet in the late-thirteenth century, and alterations to the cathedral continued to be made up until the time of its first "restoration" by Viollet-le-Duc and his collaborating architect, Jean-Baptiste Lassus, in the 1840s.

However piecemeal the appearance of a building with such a long and complex construction history might be expected to be, in fact, Notre-Dame instead seems harmonious and unified: its parts cohere in a complete picture of the Gothic. Cathedrals are sometimes likened to the image of the "Heavenly Jerusalem" as described by St. John, although the historian Otto von Simson in his fundamental study, *The Gothic Cathedral* (1956), notes that that image, in turn, was based on the Temple of Solomon as described in the Hebrew Bible. St. John, in the Book of Revelation (21:2), describes "the holy city, the new Jerusalem" descending from God in Heaven "as a bride adorned for her husband." There is nothing haphazard about this vision: the city appears complete and decked out in its finery. So too, Notre-Dame has often been described as "perfect," whole, and with its full complement of adornments in the forms of sculpture, stained glass, and precious objects. It is difficult to see past this sense of completeness to understand the long process by which the building —in a way, rather unlike St. John's vision of the bride floating down from Heaven— only gradually emerged as a vision, from the ground up.

The historical backdrop to the reconstruction of the cathedral in the mid-twelfth century is provided by Erlande-Brandenburg. He explains that the increase in the cathedral's importance took place in the late eleventh and early twelfth centuries, "when the destiny of Paris finally began to take definitive shape." Under the Capetian kings, Paris became both politically and economically more important and a new city grew up on the Roman settlement on the Right Bank. In the early twelfth century, the former cleric and archdeacon at Notre-Dame, as well as a chancellor in the royal administration between 1108 and 1127, Étienne de Garlande, spearheaded building on the Île de la Cité. In the 1120s de Garlande supported the expansion of the canon close and the construction of the surviving Chapel of Saint-Aignan along the outside of its north wall.

The Chapel of Saint-Aignan

The chapel is located on private property, to the north of Notre-Dame. The small structure, which measures about thirty-three by twenty-one feet, is vaulted and preserves some original decoration, including carved capitals based on seventh-century models. Notable here is the ongoing interweaving of new and old: the chapel was new construction, but its decoration made reference to seventh-century forms which in turn reflected classical capital designs. Following a painstaking analysis of the capitals, Lindy Grant, François Héber-Suffrin, and Danielle Valin-Johnson concluded (in the *Bulletin Monumentale*, Vol. 157, no. 3 [1999]: 283-299) that de Garlande had used his considerable political pull to employ a Burgundian sculptor to produce decorative carving for the chapel that had precedents in Cluniac monasteries but which was unknown in the Île-de-France.

Étienne de Garlande and the Renovation of Notre-Dame

Following the completion of the Chapel of Saint-Aignan, de Garlande spearheaded the renovation of the cathedral, between about 1120 and his death in 1148. When the cathedral was later rebuilt, one feature dating to de Garlande's building campaign was preserved and is still visible: the former Portal of the Virgin. The portal sculpture was saved when the cathedral was reconstructed and was reassembled, although in a somewhat different form, as the St. Anne Portal on the right (south) side of the main façade. The reuse and rededication of the portal to Christ's grandmother required its expansion (given the larger scale of the new façade) and the replacement of some sculptural figures presumably damaged during the move. The tympanum (the roughly triangular portion of sculpture above the door) depicts the Virgin seated with Christ on the Throne of Wisdom; below, the upper lintel (the horizontal band of sculpture) depicts scenes from the life of the Virgin. The figures on the right side of the lintel have been compared (in a catalogue of sculpture from Notre-Dame held at the Metropolitan Museum of Art in 1979) to sculpture on the west façade of St.-Denis, meaning that they could also date from the 1140s. Despite later destruction, replacement, and restoration of some of the figures on the door jambs, trumeau (the middle column between the two doors), and archivolts (the bands of molding that frame the tympanum), it is clear that sculpture was used on this portal in ways that mirrored the façade of St.-Denis.

The connection of Notre-Dame with St.-Denis was also made by Suger himself, who in 1150 (just before his death) donated a stained glass window, also representing the Virgin, for the cathedral. Like the portal described above, the window was saved when Notre-Dame was reconstructed and incorporated into the new construction. It survived until its accidental destruction in 1731.

Maurice de Sully and Notre-Dame

Nonetheless, as Erlande-Brandenburg observes, the completion of St.-Denis would have thrown into relief the relative modesty of Notre-Dame, despite the renovations recently made there and the introduction of new decorative features: "[...] the ancient cathedral of Paris inevitably came to seem antiquated, poorly adapted to the ambitions of its rapidly expanding diocese." Improvement of the cathedral awaited the 1160 election of Maurice de Sully as bishop whose motivations to rebuild were not purely pragmatic. As his early biographer, Victor Mortet wrote in 1890, "He wished to commemorate his episcopate by building a sumptuous cathedral." De Sully's project went beyond architecture: he emphasized the role of the cathedral in serving the entire diocese and to do so, created twelve parishes on the island, each with its own parish church. Moreover, because the footprint of the cathedral was to be increased —to about 59,000 square feet in a building measuring 131 feet across and 402 feet long— the site had to be reorganized. Making a very large building on the densely-built island entailed certain challenges; moreover, de Sully's conception of the cathedral in its setting was new. He intended to create an open *parvis* in front of the west façade. Thus, the new cathedral was located approximately 130 feet east of the earlier building, other structures to the east (located on church property) were demolished, and the east end of the island expanded by landfill. The square in front of the cathedral would be accessed by a new east-west street, the rue Neuve-Notre-Dame, which archaeologist Jacques Nicourt argued was created by aligning some existing streets with the new orientation of the cathedral. Given that the previous cathedral was only demolished on a piecemeal basis as the new one took shape, the *parvis* would not actually exist as a physical space for decades.

The relocation and reorientation of the cathedral necessitated as well the demolition of nearby houses (following protracted negotiations with their owners) and of the Hôtel Dieu, or charity hospital, which had been located in front of the old cathedral. Its new location was outside of the ancient fortifications and close to the river, to the southwest of the new cathedral. Construction was begun in 1163 and continued for about a century. Directly south of the cathedral —between it and the Seine— de Sully erected a new bishop's palace that replaced an earlier, more modest "residence" of the bishop. It consisted of a two-story building with a hall at the west end and a chapel at the east; a tower rose from an interior court. Surviving drawings (the palace was later destroyed, as we will see) show that its south side was buttressed and culminated in crenellation at the roofline.

The bishop's palace was balanced on the north side of the cathedral by the chapter close —that precinct under control of the cathedral for the use of its canons, or clergy. In 1165, as de Sully's project was taking shape, Pope Alexander III "reaffirmed the chapter's property holdings and privileges." Erlande-Brandenburg describes the close in the fourteenth century as comprising "thirty-seven residences, each endowed with a plot of land and an annuity." Other residences occupied by the clergy were located outside the close as was the small church of

St.-Denis-du-Pas, mentioned previously, which was demolished in 1815. The close expanded through the eighteenth century to include additional houses and gardens, along with other buildings, including the so-called Dagobert Tower which survived until 1909.

During his episcopate of thirty-six years, which lasted until his death in 1196, de Sully was able to bring to fruition a substantial portion of his vision for a new cathedral in a reconfigured setting. Over that span of years, de Sully saw the rue Neuve-Notre-Dame cut through the island's built fabric, the hospital relocated, a new bishop's palace constructed, and with regard to the cathedral itself, the new choir dedicated and the nave begun. Moreover, he set in motion the realization of his grand conception for the cathedral that was carried on after his death. All of this building required money. While private donations may have funded the reconstruction of the Hôtel Dieu, de Sully personally paid for the new bishop's palace. De Sully lacked a large personal fortune, but he —like Suger before him— was a skillful administrator and was able to marshal those funds to which he had access as bishop to pursue the projects he envisioned.

The Gothic Architect

De Sully's administrative skills, and those of his unknown architect, would have been required to address the substantial practical considerations that a building project of this scale would have entailed. In fact, at just the time of Notre-Dame's reconstruction, according to architectural historian Spiro Kostof (in *The Architect: Chapters in the History of the Profession*, 2000) the concept of the architect in the West was in transition. He had come to be thought of less as the classical "humanist planner" and more as a "master-builder." Between 800 and 1150 the conception of the architect developed just when "a distinctly medieval architecture with its own iconography and building techniques had come to full bloom;" subsequently, "the Gothic period […] in form as well as in the approach to the architect's profession introduced and nurtured a fresh tradition." There was no official school in which the architects of Gothic buildings trained; rather, they began as apprentices to older practitioners while still in their teens, followed that experience with a period as a journeyman, and finally obtained some training on the job. All the while, "the architect found the chance to intermingle with the upper classes and absorb their learned ways." Intellectual sophistication was required to produce the design for the building, alongside the more practical knowledge of construction provided during the years of traineeship. Drawings from the later Middle Ages show that architects also needed graphic abilities to convey their concepts to patrons and workers, and at the same time, they required administrative skill to organize a vast workshop of laborers, skilled craftsmen, and artists. The rapid pace of construction in Paris suggests that the construction crew there was large, and the sheer scale of the project meant that materials —particularly wood and stone— had to be aggressively sought out and their transportation to the site organized.

A paucity of documentation for Notre-Dame in this period precludes a specific description of the building process, but, as Erlande-Brandenburg points out, the progress was relatively rapid. By the time of the consecration of the new high altar, on May 19, 1182, "the entirety of the building's eastern portion was complete, including vaults, stained-glass windows, an ecclesiastical furniture, notably stalls for the canons."

The enormous scale of Notre-Dame had both civic and religious significance: "This giganticism must have been intended as an assertion of the pre-eminence of Paris among the cities of the kingdom and also as a demonstration of the status of the mother church of a city where many churches had been rebuilt recently" (Wilson). Notre-Dame maintained the same proportions of width to height as in the projected nave and transept at St.-Denis, which was 1:2.5, but the cathedral of Paris was about a third higher, at thirty-three meters. The choir of Notre-

Dame also continued the use of massive columns in its first-story arcade, to support six-part groin vaults above, in the manner seen earlier at St.-Denis. Wilson speculates that historic references may have been made in this enormous modern building, as in others of its kind, to the earlier columned basilicas that were being replaced. In line with St.-Denis, the choir wall was treated as a thin membrane, opened with expanses of glass.

De Sully's vision for the enormous light-filled vessel of the church persisted even after the first architect was succeeded by the second before 1182 or possibly as early as 1177, two decades or more before de Sully's death. Prior to that point, the old apse had started to be replaced and the west façade begun, with the idea that the western and eastern portions of the new cathedral would be joined to complete the building. This second architect is believed to have died around 1200 when a new, third architect replaced him. Under his direction the façade was begun and the work on the nave suspended. When he got to the balustrade above the Gallery of Kings, he turned to joining the two blocks of the building which Erlande-Brandenburg suggests took place under Maurice de Sully's successor —Eudes de Sully— who died in 1208. Initially, the interior would have been protected by the wood-supported lead roof —the one lost to the fire of April 15, 2019— but the stone vaults above the nave would not have been finished. Andrew Tallon observes that the contemporary chronicler Robert de Torigny noted that the choir at Notre-Dame was completed "excepto majori tectoria," that is, "except for the great covering," or vaults, by 1177.

Shortly thereafter (c. 1210 to 1220), a fourth architect took over, completing the joining of the façade block and nave. He continued the construction of the nave walls and vaulting, and also introduced changes to the west façade which included expanding the size of the rose window. In 1220 the sculpted figures of the Gallery of Kings on the west façade were installed and by 1245 the two towers at the façade were completed to their current level. In contrast to other Gothic churches and cathedrals, spires were not added to them.

The Architects of Notre-Dame and the Rayonnant Gothic Style

Changes were made to the existing building starting in the 1220s. Originally, the choir and nave elevations were four stories in height with a gallery above the arcade, surmounted by circular windows, and above those, a clerestory level. A little more than a half-century after the consecration of the main altar, between about 1230 and 1240, the interior elevation was reworked by removing the circular windows and earlier clerestory and inserting new, longer clerestory windows. The four-story elevation thereby became a three-story elevation. (In the nineteenth century, as we will see, the original four-story design was partially restored.) Around the same time, the construction of the chapels between the buttresses was likely begun, with the earlier ones, on the north side of the nave, dating to around 1235-40. Around 1250 the north and south facades of the transept were constructed. We know the identities of the architects of these parts of the building. The older, north façade was the work of architect Jean de Chelles (b. 1200) who, before his death, laid the foundation of the later, south façade in 1258. De Chelles was succeeded as architect at Notre-Dame by Pierre de Montreuil (d. 1267) whom Anne Prache credits with having refined the Parisian Rayonnant Gothic style of the thirteenth century, characterized by unified compositions of masonry elements and light-filled interiors. According to Erlande-Brandenberg's building chronology (in the *Grove Dictionary of Art*), in the fourteenth century the work of de Chelles was continued by Jean Ravy who enlarged the gallery windows in the chevet and installed flying buttresses.

The history of the flying buttresses at Notre-Dame has been the subject of scholarly debate since the nineteenth century. Andrew J. Tallon, using a computer controlled laser, recently undertook exact measurements of the structure to determine precisely its history of construction. A commonly held belief was that flying buttresses had first been used on the nave at Notre-Dame and that therefore the choir (constructed earlier) must not have had them originally. However, more recent research —including Tallon's computer-aided analysis— suggests instead that the choir was intended to have flying buttresses from the time that construction began in the 1160s. Tallon's imaging of Notre-Dame constitutes the most reliable representation of the structure in existence and is being used as the current restoration of the cathedral proceeds. The flying buttresses are one of the most recognized elements of Notre-Dame's Rayonnant Gothic structure and they are also one of the features most touched by cycles of neglect and restoration —some would say over-restoration. In his essay, "Rethinking Medieval Structure," Tallon makes this point by referring to what he calls the "draconian formal homogenization [perpetrated] by Lassus and Viollet-le-Duc" on the fabric of Notre-Dame.

Had the mid-nineteenth century restoration of the cathedral been less sweeping, Notre-Dame would still be a building that represented multiple visions —and revisions— of its "complete" form. As the long and complicated history of its construction demonstrates, the cathedral is the precise opposite of the modern stereotype of a massive building project, one in which a single-minded patron provides the material means to bring to life the design concept developed by a lone architect-genius. Instead, the Gothic building grew on the foundations laid by earlier structures, its form changed in subtle as well as in major ways over the years when it was being constructed, and it was being revised even before it was finished. Indeed, for all of its centuries-long history Notre-Dame de Paris has always been embroiled in a dynamic process of making and remaking.

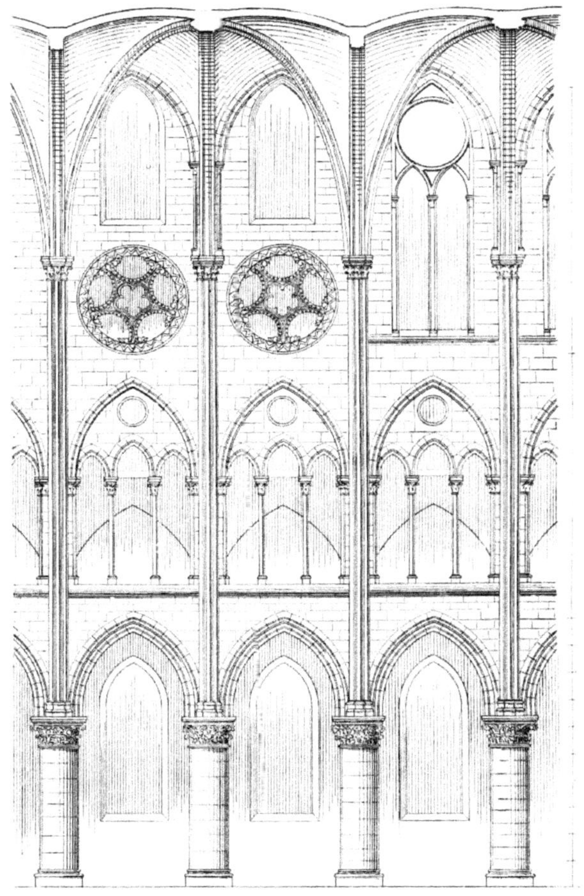

7. Viollet-le-Duc's drawing intended to show two original bays of the nave and one as altered during the thirteenth century.

Chapter 3

Gothic Paris

The Gothic beyond Notre-Dame

Although Notre-Dame may be the largest and most famous Gothic building in Paris, it is not the only one. In fact, in relatively close proximity to the cathedral are found a number of churches dating from the Middle Ages that represent various stages in the development of Gothic architecture. And beyond the city itself, elsewhere in the Île-de-France region, are many other examples that help to place Notre-Dame in its historical and architectural context. From this perspective, the cathedral of Notre-Dame occupies a significant, yet complicated, position. The production of Gothic architecture lasted for centuries, and as the examples located within a twenty-minute walk of Notre-Dame demonstrate, it had many different expressions, some of which are recognized as subcategories of the Gothic, like the Rayonnant style or the Flamboyant style. Central Paris offers a virtual compendium of medieval Gothic buildings that not infrequently bear some relationship to Notre-Dame, the undeniably dominant example in the city.

The study of Gothic architecture cut its teeth on the churches and cathedrals of the Île-de-France. From the time of the first concentrated antiquarian study of medieval architecture in the nineteenth century, the great monuments of north central France were considered the "gold standard" by which Gothic architecture in other regions and countries was judged —fairly or not. A group of Gothic ecclesiastical buildings was identified by antiquarians and later by historians to illustrate the ostensible "progression" of the style, from its origins at St. Denis to the achievement of the High Gothic in the cathedrals of Chartres, Reims, and Amiens —all located in the Île-de-France. In addition to being considered architecturally significant, these buildings were also thought of as the very embodiment of French culture and as harbingers of historical memory. As the American novelist Edith Wharton observed of Amiens cathedral in her travelogue, *A Motor-Flight Through France* (1906): "A great Gothic cathedral sums up so much of history, it has cost so much in faith and toil, in blood and folly and saintly abnegation, it has sheltered such a long succession of lives, given collective voice to so many inarticulate and contradictory cravings, seen so much that was sublime and terrible, or foolish, pitiful and grotesque, that it is like some mysteriously preserved ancestor of the human race, some Wandering Jew grown sedentary and throned in stony contemplation, before whom the fleeting generations come and go." Imposing, venerable, and venerated Gothic monuments were considered to be intimately connected to the development of the French nation through the Middle Ages.

The Church of St.-Germain-des-Prés

The political history of France, as well as its cultural achievements, is amply represented in the Gothic buildings of Paris. Not far from Notre-Dame, on the Left Bank, the Frankish King Childebert founded the monastic church of St.-Vincent and Sainte-Croix in the sixth century as a royal burial place with one of its major relics being the tunic of Saint Vincent. Later, the church's dedication was changed to honor Saint Germain (496-576) the bishop of Paris who, as scholar Nirmal Dass explains, encouraged Childebert to give up "worldly pleasures" and focus instead on piety while eradicating persistent pagan practices in Gaul. After Childebert's death in 558, Saint Germain worked to quell civil war among the king's possible successors. Saint Germain was buried in the church of St.-Vincent and Sainte-Croix, and later he was reinterred there and the church was rededicated in his honor. Originally constructed outside the city walls, St.-Germain-des-Prés was also named to indicate its location, since the word "Prés" here refers to the meadows that were found near the church at the time of its dedication. On this site, the present church of St.-Germain-des-Prés was constructed in the Rayonnant style during the eleventh and twelfth centuries.

According to art historian William Clark, the dedication ceremony, held in 1163 with Pope Alexander III in attendance, coincided with the completion of a new chevet as well as tombs for Childebert and his family. Clark explains in an article published in the *Journal of the Society of Architectural Historians* (Vol. 38, no. 4 [Dec. 1979]: 348-65) that the choir is usually thought to have been inspired by the early Gothic church of St.-Denis and that it comprises three parts: an ambulatory, chapels, and choir. The twelfth-century chevet was integrated with the eleventh-century nave and transept which were in turn built on the foundations of the earlier church on the site. Indeed, a blending of new and old features is one of the major characteristics of St.-Germain-des-Prés. The nine chapels of the chevet are entered through round-arched openings (often associated with the Romanesque style) while their vaults are supported by pointed-arched ribbed vaults, characteristic of the Gothic mode. In contrast, the arcades of the ambulatory are comprised of massive columns supporting heavy round arches —forms used extensively in Romanesque churches and even earlier, in Roman basilicas. In the central portion of the choir, argues Clark, the mixing of new and old elements is even more pronounced than elsewhere in the chevet, but "differences between the two are minimized." For instance, in the second story of the chevet small columns or colonnettes divide each major opening in half. The capitals and bases of these colonnettes were carved in the twelfth century, but they combine seamlessly with the shafts of the columns, made of marble, which were either reused from the sixth-century church on the site, or were made new but intended to look like survivals, or "spolia," from the earlier building. Clark suggests that the colonnettes were meant to represent the ongoing investment of the royalty in the church and to rival the contemporary chevet built by the Abbot Suger at St.-Denis.

Despite seventeenth-century alterations to St.-Germain-des-Prés, as well as decorative painting that dates to the nineteenth century (to which we will turn below), the original "unified" spatial character of the choir is still visible. While the conception of the interior responded to Suger's innovations at St.-Denis, the exterior of St.-Germain-des-Prés tells us that its builders were aware of what was being constructed nearby at Notre-Dame. In particular, the flying buttresses around the chevet are thought to date to later in the twelfth century and to have not been anticipated in the original design of the east end of St.-Germain-des-Prés, meaning that they were not considered structurally essential. They may have been inspired by similar elements under way at Notre-Dame. In turn, Clark considers that the spatial sophistication of the smaller St.-Germain-des-Prés was important for its neighbor that loomed on the Île de la Cité: "The aesthetic direction of the choir space of Saint-Germain-des-Prés was continued in the colossal grandeur of Notre-Dame, Paris, with its contrast between the enormous size of that space and the delicacy of the parts that define it."

The Painting of St.-Germain-des-Prés

The visitor to St.-Germain-des-Prés today might well overlook its architectural and spatial qualities and instead focus on the incredible decorative richness that has been enhanced by a recent restoration of its interior painting. In 2018, a non-profit organization, the American Friends for the Preservation of Saint-Germain-des-Prés, was established to support the ongoing preservation of the church. The project was directed toward the restoration of painting originally carried out by artist Hippolyte Flandrin (1809-64), his brother Paul Flandrin (1811-1902), and his student Sébastien Cornu (1804-70), beginning in 1842. From that point until his death, Flandrin was occupied at St.-Germain-des-Prés with the production of numerous large-scale paintings using the encaustic (wax-based) technique he had used in earlier commissions. In addition to such scenes from the Old and New Testaments as the *Entry of Christ into Jerusalem* and the *Adoration of the Magi*, the interior also displays extensive decorative painting, in brilliant colors and rich gold. Notably, in the Gothic nave and choir, the vaults are painted bright blue with gold stars, and the supporting ribs are picked out in gold and red.

Pierre de Montreuil, one-time master of the works at Notre-Dame, is known to have built the refectory at St.-Germain-des-Prés between 1239 and 1244 and the Lady Chapel from 1245 to c.1250. Only fragments of de Montreuil's work at St.-Germain-des-Prés survive, since the refectory was largely destroyed in 1797 and the chapel in 1802, but the sheer involvement of this pioneering architect at the monastery suggests the importance of the building. These works also contributed to the spread of a new and particularly Parisian version of the Gothic —the Rayonnant. It reflected the growth of Paris during the period in terms of both population and wealth.

The Sainte-Chapelle

Rivalling St.-Germain-des-Prés as a richly decorated, painted Gothic interior is the Sainte-Chapelle, located even closer to Notre-Dame on the Île de la Cité. Its construction in the 1240s followed the development of the Rayonnant style at St.-Denis where in 1231 Abbot Eudes Clément spearheaded the replacement of the surviving Carolingian nave (which at that point would have been flanked by the rebuilt early Gothic west end and the choir to the east, both masterminded by Suger) with a more modern version. The unidentified architect of the new nave at St.-Denis distinguished between Suger's earlier choir and his own intervention by dispensing with the single columns that appeared in the choir and substituting for them complex supporting piers that, if they were sliced through at ground level, would be cruciform in shape. These piers were bundles of vertical elements that soared to the vaults above, past the walls that were opened up with stained glass framed by elaborate tracery. The feeling of a thin-skinned, light-filled vessel that the viewer experiences in the nave at St.-Denis is similarly felt at the Sainte-Chapelle.

Neither an abbey church (associated with a monastery) nor a cathedral (connected with a bishop), the Sainte-Chapelle had a very special function: it was built by King Louis IX (1214-70) to house an extremely important relic, the reputed Crown of Thorns. This sacred object was purchased from the Byzantine Emperor Baldwin II and brought to Paris in 1239. The building, which rose as part of the palace complex on the east end of the Île de la Cité, was so closely connected with the patronage of Louis IX —later "Saint" Louis— that it was long considered a prime example of his "Court Style." In her definitive monograph, *The Sainte-Chapelle and the Construction of Sacral Monarchy* (2015), architectural historian Meredith Cohen explains that instead of the "Court Style," "During the thirteenth century, the style of Gothic architecture made in Paris was called *opere francigeno* ('French work')" because it was closely associated with the monarchy which underwrote the construction of many examples of what is now commonly termed the Rayonnant style. Moreover, Cohen states that the Sainte-Chapelle represented a shift away from the "unadorned and functional" architecture built by Louis IX's predecessor, King Philip Augustus (1165-1223), towards a much more decorative expression of royal authority.

The Sainte-Chapelle comprises two stories, of which the upper is higher and more light-filled with soaring stained-glass windows at both sides. The floor plan consists of four bays, or sections, at each level, as well as a porch, and an apse. At the first story, the chapel's vaulted ceiling is relatively low in comparison to the upper level but still the feeling of openness in the space is maximized. At the upper story, the space is similarly unified as a result of the structural elements being pushed to the periphery in order to maximize the expansiveness of the spatial experience. What is most impressive about the upper-level space is, however, its decorative richness. Cohen summarizes the experience of Sainte-Chapelle as "less rational and more mystical": "The brilliant colors of the stained-glass windows, the glow of the gilding, the opposing harmonies of the polychromed surfaces (red/blue, yellow/green) enhance this effect." The color scheme of the interior is believed to be close to the original treatment although it was heavily restored in the nineteenth century.

The Church of Saint Séverin and the Flamboyant Gothic

Close by on the Left Bank another, comparatively smaller, Gothic church rose over the course of several centuries, dedicated to Saint Séverin, or Saint Severinus (d. c. 540), a devout hermit who was said to have lived on the banks of the Seine. The church's tangled construction history has been explained by Andrew Ayers (in *The Architecture of Paris: an Architectural Guide*, 2004). A church was on the site from the sixth century, but its appearance owes far more to its subsequent rebuilding, first in the early thirteenth century when its importance to the Left Bank community demanded expansion. It was a simple eight-bay building that had a flat east end as opposed to the developed chevet seen in other Gothic churches. It was subsequently enlarged, although little remains of these early building campaigns. Most significant for its present appearance was the reconstruction that lasted nearly a century and that followed a fire at St.-Séverin in 1448. Just before 1500, the choir was rebuilt and included the celebrated ambulatory; its most famous element is a twisted column at the ambulatory's center —on axis with the entrance— from which fourteen vault ribs spring. Sometimes compared to a palm tree, this column has attracted numerous photographers, printmakers, and painters who have depicted it over the course of centuries.

In his classic monograph on *Art and Architecture in Medieval France* (2018, originally published as *Monastery and Cathedral in France*, 1972), Whitney Stoddard compared the cathedral at Chartres with the church of St.-Séverin to illustrate the distinction between the High Gothic (at Chartres) and the Late, or Flamboyant Gothic (at St.-Séverin) styles. Stoddard points to the way that the ribs of the vaults emerge from the piers supporting the ambulatory at St.-Séverin, as well as the famed twisted column, as being distinctive from the use of capitals at the tops of the columns and piers in earlier Gothic interiors. The twisting forms of various elements of the St.-Séverin interior create a sense of dynamic movement, and emphasize effects of light and shade in a way that contrasts with the staid effects of early and High Gothic churches. Inside, St.-Séverin is more "pictorial" and "expressive" than its earlier counterparts. The Decadent writer Joris-Karl Huysmans (1848-1907) perhaps did the most to promote a view of St.-Séverin's interior as dynamic, having described in his book *La Bièvre et Saint-Séverin* (1898) the twisted ambulatory column as being like a tree that supports a "petrified rain of branches" (vault ribs). A short walk from Notre-Dame to the Left Bank thus allows us to observe the development of the early Gothic and the Rayonnant style (in the cathedral and in the Sainte-Chapelle) and finally the Flamboyant style at St.-Séverin.

The Church of St.-Germain-l'Auxerrois

On the Right Bank, not far from Notre-Dame, is another Gothic building with as long and complicated a construction history as St.-Séverin's: the church of St.-Germain-l'Auxerrois, located just to the east of the Louvre. It too occupies the site of a much earlier religious building, thought to date from the late sixth century, and it was rebuilt between the twelfth and sixteenth centuries. For our purposes, the most significant of these projects was the rebuilding that began in the thirteenth century, when a new plan was modeled on that of Notre-Dame. So, the choir was designed to be longer than the nave, and ended in an apse with an ambulatory, as at the cathedral. The transepts of St.-Germain-l'Auxerrois did not project beyond the sides of the nave —also a distinctive feature of Notre-Dame's plan. From a later reconstruction is the rose window of the west façade, in the Flamboyant style. Like St.-Germain-des-Prés, St.-Germain-l'Auxerrois was thought to have been patronized by King Childebert and its generally royal associations —which also resulted from its location next to the Louvre palace— made the church a target for destruction during the French Revolution of the late eighteenth century. In 1831 it was again "pillaged and left standing a ruin" (according to J. Steward, *The Stranger's Guide to Paris*, 1837), as the result of politically-motivated destruction. Nonetheless, parts of the building dating to its Gothic past still survive.

The rose window of St.-Germain-l'Auxerrois is among the most noteworthy Gothic survivals in the church, and was mimicked in the adjoining Mairie (or City Hall) of the First Arrondissement which was built between 1857 and 1864 to the design of architect Jacques-Ignace Hittorff (1792-1867). It was intended as a remedy to what was felt to be an unattractive lack of symmetry in the public square in front of the Louvre. The cue for the design came from the church which had just been restored (1839-55) by one of the architects of the nearly contemporary Notre-Dame restoration: Jean-Baptiste Lassus. Just a few years later, between 1858 and 1861, a Flamboyant-style tower was built between the church and the Mairie, after a design by architect Théodore Ballu. The nineteenth-century construction adjacent to the church was not well received. As early as 1891 (July 11th), *The Churchman* opined that "If we could for a moment clear away the towers and buildings which hem it in, we should be able to better see and admire the enchanting entrance and front of St.-Germain-l'Auxerrois, as it stands cloaked and hidden on all sides and forbidding any clear view of its superb perspectives." Despite this occlusion, the church stood as a monument to the development of Gothic architecture from the twelfth through the fourteenth centuries (and possibly beyond) and to its ongoing importance as a model for new building.

The Church of St.-Eustache: Gothic Survival

Our selective tour of Paris's Gothic monuments concludes with a late example that suggests the growing importance of classical architectural forms in France from the sixteenth century onward: the church of St.-Eustache, built between 1532 and 1640. Located close to Paris's central market district, St.-Eustache possessed many elements that recalled the cathedral of Notre-Dame, not far off on the Île de la Cité, but built centuries earlier. Although it is only half the height of Notre-Dame (about 100 feet as opposed to 226 feet), St.-Eustache still rises above most of the surrounding buildings and that prominence would have been even more pronounced at the time of its original construction. Besides its visual dominance, other aspects of St.-Eustache also tie it to earlier Gothic buildings. It has a familiar plan with double aisles on each side leading to an ambulatory that encircles the choir at the east end, and the transepts do not project beyond the perimeter of the nave, as at Notre-Dame. On the interior, the nave elevation has an extremely high first-story arcade that accentuates the verticality of the sanctuary, as do the pilasters (or flattened columns) and colonnettes that run up the arcade's piers and culminate in ribbed vaults. The pattern of ribs is complex and decorative; it is consistent with very late examples of the Gothic style constructed elsewhere on the Continent and in Great Britain. On the exterior of St.-Eustache the nave and choir are supported by flying buttresses, a trademark element of Gothic architecture, and one that is especially prominent at nearby Notre-Dame.

While it was never difficult for observers to pick out the Gothic parts of St.-Eustache, many were hard pressed to explain the presence of what seemed to be classical elements —such as the pilasters mentioned above— in a building modeled on medieval precedents. One of many such commentaries came from Marius Vachon who, in 1910, wrote of St.-Eustache that "on a skeleton that is entirely Gothic, with traditional architectural schemas, they toss, in a charming caprice of the imagination, a Renaissance garment and adornment." By separating the Gothic structure from the classical ornament, critics suggested that in the sixteenth century, French architects were relying on their tradition of masterful construction in stone (that went back to the Middle Ages) while simultaneously looking to the classical forms that were just then being rediscovered by Italian Renaissance artists.

The church of St.-Eustache demonstrates the persistence of Notre-Dame, and of the Gothic tradition more generally, in French architecture through to the modern period. The Gothic sensibility that can be observed in St.-Eustache was a "survival" from earlier times; in subsequent chapters we will see how, by the nineteenth century, there was a considered and concerted "revival" of the Gothic in France, as there was throughout the West. In Paris, the restoration of Notre-Dame in the mid- to late-nineteenth century was a major catalyst for the revival. The impact of the cathedral of Notre-Dame was inescapable.

Gothic Revival and the Church of St.-Jean-de-Montmartre

The influence of Notre-Dame's most important restoration architect, Viollet-le-Duc, was as pervasive in Paris and beyond as the "original" cathedral had been during the Middle Ages. In the capital itself, there are a number of neo-Gothic churches that demonstrate how the restoration of Notre-Dame contributed to the popularity of the medieval style as a model for new religious buildings. For instance, the direct impact of Viollet-le-Duc can be seen in the church of St.-Jean-de-Montmartre, built between 1894 and 1904 and designed by the architect Anatole de Baudot (1834-1915), a student of Viollet-le-Duc's. Starting in 1863, de Baudot and Viollet-le-Duc directed the journal, the *Gazette des Architectes et du Bâtiment* (*Gazette of Architects and Building*) where de Baudot echoed some of his teacher's concepts of the Gothic, including the claim that the major objective of medieval builders had been to construct large, open spaces. In St.-Jean-de-Montmartre, de Baudot gave material form to Viollet-le-Duc's point that the Gothic could guide new building, not by providing models to follow slavishly, but instead by suggesting principles that contemporary architects could adapt. The modern relevance of the Gothic, Viollet-le-Duc argued, derived from the fact that medieval masons had proceeded much in the manner of contemporary engineers, by pushing the capacities of stone construction to their limits, as was especially evident in the largest churches and cathedrals of the Middle Ages.

Thus, at St.-Jean-de-Montmartre, de Baudot used contemporary materials to create a large, soaring space. On the interior, the reinforced concrete structural system developed by de Baudot and the young engineer Paul Cottancin (1865 – 1928), made it possible to echo the Gothic in new and relatively inexpensive materials. Architectural historian Kenneth Frampton explains the construction system, in his book, *Studies in Tectonic Culture* (1995): "Cottancin's ciment armé [reinforced concrete] employed wire-reinforced, perforated brickwork as the permanent framework of a cement armature, together with thin, lightweight cement shells [...] the wire reinforcement and cement infill were considered as acting independently, the former in tension the latter in compression." The cement shells gave the appearance of Gothic stone vaults, making a connection to medieval architecture which was furthered by the incorporation of stained glass throughout the interior. On the exterior, the paired stained glass windows that soar above the central portal refer visually to Gothic churches and cathedrals like Notre-Dame, while the prominent towers underscore how important restored medieval buildings continued to be as models for modern designers of religious buildings, even into the twentieth century.

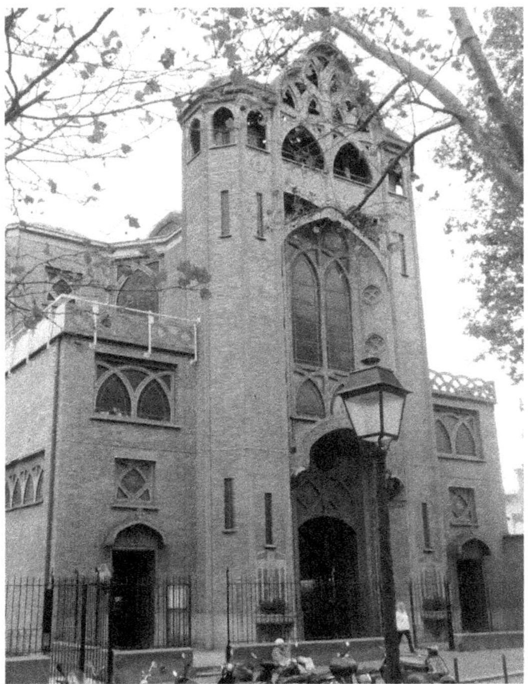

8. St-Jean-de-Montmartre.

Chapter 4

Notre-Dame and Political Revolution

Gothic Architecture and Politics

Architecture is almost always a social and political art. Rarely are buildings constructed in complete isolation and the process of making them is almost never a solitary undertaking. Erecting an enormous and costly building like a Gothic cathedral often could not be undertaken without support from the monarchy or other wealthy patrons, and of course, without church support. From the outset then, a Gothic church or cathedral often found itself at the nexus of church and state, and that situation did not change over the course of succeeding centuries. A church or cathedral from the Middle Ages, however architecturally splendid it might be, could only survive if either secular or religious institutions (or both) provided the funds to maintain it. So, these historic monuments were at the mercy of the shifting fortunes of church and state. Furthermore, their fundamental connections with the Catholic church and with the monarchy or nobility put them in the crosshairs of revolutionaries in 1789 and beyond.

The politicization of medieval monuments had implications for their material fabric. Sometimes churches and cathedrals were deliberately damaged as a way of symbolically opposing the current political regime; at others, they were simply disused and their maintenance was neglected. Eventually, the most extraordinary examples, such as Notre-Dame, were restored as "historic monuments."

Over the course of centuries in which Gothic buildings were at the receiving end of —in alternation— conservation and destruction, they registered the changing political situation in their very fabric. Signs of decay or deliberate damage were considered to be blemishes that marred their original appearances, but they were also badges of honor —flaws that attested to a building's durability and resilience. Obviously the product of lavish expenditures of money and labor, medieval churches and cathedrals readily drew both the ire of critics and the praise of the faithful. Very few nineteenth-century observers of Gothic churches and cathedrals were neutral, but whatever their opinions, they all recognized the significance of the buildings as witnesses to the unfolding of French history.

Revolutionary "Vandalism" and the Gothic

The royal patronage of Notre-Dame, and of other Gothic churches and cathedrals, as well as the historic association of the French monarchy with the Catholic church, meant that the French Revolution of the late eighteenth century would target the church and its buildings, just as it did the King and his family, the aristocracy, and the buildings connected with both. An order of November 2, 1789 brought about the nationalization of church property and eventually led to the deliberate removal of religious and royal symbolism from public buildings. Both of these developments had implications for Notre-Dame de Paris.

The Revolutionary Convention, in 1792, issued a series of orders directing the removal of signs of the royalty from buildings, official seals, and military uniforms. However, as early as 1793 the Assembly urged restraint in the removal of such symbols and cautioned that while "crowns, fleurs de Lys, arms and other signs of the royalty" could be taken off of sculpted busts and monuments, "the rest [the underlying objects] should be preserved as necessary to the arts and to the decoration of monuments."

Thus, although the reviled symbols of the monarchy and the clergy were to be suppressed, there was still respect in Revolutionary France for works of art that transcended the circumstances under which they had been produced. So too for architecture. In the spring of 1792, a Commission Conservatrice des Monuments (Monuments Conservation Commission) was established in Paris. This body was supposed to oversee the obliteration of signs of the monarchy and church while also preventing the destruction of significant works of art and architecture. By late 1793, the Commission Temporaire des Arts (Temporary Commission of the Arts) was established to inventory the French artistic and architectural patrimony that had come into public hands through nationalization. One of the measures proposed by the commission was the establishment of a national body to keep a watchful gaze all over France for places where historic monuments were still threatened by a "destructive furor."

"Vandalisme"

This furious will to destroy the iconography of the institutions of the *ancien régime* (the pre-Revolutionary period) was widely referred to as "vandalisme." Historians have noted that it existed side-by-side with preservation efforts, as Michel Beurdeley has written (in an article entitled "Le Vandalisme Révolutionnaire," 1989): "On the one hand, [the Revolutionary authority] wants to preserve cultural goods from destruction. [...] But [supported] by ideology and opportunism it does not hesitate to sell royal furniture abroad, to destroy statues, to throw onto the flames, mountains of feudal emblems and to melt down church bells [...]." The most vocal and influential critic of Revolutionary vandalism came from the church. He was the Abbé Henri Jean-Baptiste Grégoire (1750-1831) who, in three reports to the National Convention in 1794, argued that vandalism was a counter-revolutionary activity that robbed France of its history and impoverished the learning of its people. In his memoirs published in 1837, the Abbé Grégoire wrote, "Le vandalisme. Je créai le mot pour tuer la chose." ("Vandalism. I created the word to kill the thing.")

The Revolution put buildings and monuments that had been constructed by banished institutions in the hands of bodies with little sympathy for them, except as works of art and architecture that expressed a French national "genius" transcending political and religious affiliations. Moreover, the nationalization of the property belonging to the church, monarchy, and nobility created a surplus of buildings, especially since Catholic practice had been outlawed. François Souchal observes in his comprehensive study of *Le Vandalisme de la Révolution* (1993) that the Revolutionary authorities found there to be an overabundance of churches on the Île de la Cité: seventeen in all, of which only Notre-Dame and the Sainte-Chapelle survive. The rest, Souchal suggests, were lost to demolition or conversion to new uses.

The survivors were prominent elements of the Parisian landscape and also key sites for both the church and the monarchy; hence they were targeted for vandalism. The Sainte-Chapelle, for instance, had its spire removed, leaving a hole in the roof that gaped open for three months, endangering the survival of the building. Moreover, the mayor of Paris, Jean-Nicolas Pache, initiated a debate on the possible demolition of Sainte-Chapelle on the grounds that "from top to bottom it is covered with royal symbols." In the end, rather than demolish it, the chapel was converted to new use as a repository for archives and the sculpted figures of apostles were removed from the columns of the upper chapel, breaking two of them in the process. Some of the original stained glass was lost as well.

Of obvious symbolic significance, Notre-Dame was an inevitable object of Revolutionary vandalism. At first, in 1792, precious objects were removed from the treasury by night. In conformance with official directives, the crowns were also ordered removed from the heads of twenty-eight figures of the Kings of Judea and Israel located on the west façade. The Gallery of Kings would come in for complete destruction as the extent of vandalism increased over the course of the Revolution. Thus, on the twenty-third of October, 1793, the Council of the City of Paris ordered that in view of "its obligation to vanish all monuments that feed religious prejudices and those that recall the execrable memory of kings, orders that within a week, the Gothic simulacra of the kings of France, that are placed above the portal of the church of Notre-Dame, be removed and destroyed." A contractor named Varin was charged with removing the figures one by one (and he reused the materials in construction projects). Some say that the Biblical kings from the façade of Notre-Dame were confused with representations of the kings of France, which ignited the rage of the mob that had assembled to watch their destruction. The report that the sculptures were beheaded as they came down is supported by the fact that twenty-one of the original twenty-eight heads were excavated in 1977. At that time, 300 other fragments of sculpture were found entombed in the foundations of Notre-Dame. Those likely resulted from the battering of much of the rest of the exterior sculpture, from which the figure of the Virgin on the trumeau of the portal at the north crossing escaped. The interior of Notre-Dame, reports Souchal, was virtually emptied when it was converted to use as a "Temple of Reason" in 1793.

While decapitating sculptures of kings is a clear act of symbolic destruction, the demolition of the spire of Notre-Dame could be understood as both symbolic and practical. For one thing, structural issues with the thirteenth-century spire had been noted prior to 1789, so it was already in distress before the adherents of the Revolution began targeting buildings and monuments associated with the church and monarchy. The order given by the Revolutionary government to take down the spire in 1792 may also have been motivated by a need for the lead which covered it. Once the spire was down, it would not be replaced for more than sixty years, and then by one based on a new design by Viollet-le-Duc.

Napoléon and Notre-Dame

The regime of Napoléon I, who was crowned Emperor of France at Notre-Dame in 1804, brought about the repair of some damage to the cathedral but failed to produce a full-fledged restoration of the building. In 1810 a modest annual maintenance budget for Notre-Dame, which had been suspended during the Revolution, was reestablished. Napoléon also provided a salary for the archbishop of Paris and the maintenance of his residence, and a chapter of monks was formed at the cathedral. Following the collapse of the Empire, in 1814-1815, the Bourbon monarchy was restored under King Louis XVIII, and then under his successor Charles X who reigned from 1824 until the July Revolution of 1830. Given the Revolutionary destruction of parts of Notre-Dame, as well as deferred maintenance during the period in which Catholic religious practice was abolished, some work was required to prevent further harm to the cathedral during the Empire. It was largely carried out by architects trained in the classical tradition and will be discussed in the next chapter. During the Restoration monarchy as well as the early July Monarchy of King Louis-Philippe which followed it, the clergy advocated for the repair of Notre-Dame to make it functional for religious practice, since the Concordat of 1801 between Napoléon and Pope Pius VII reinstated Catholicism in France, albeit under the authority of the state.

Throughout the first three decades of the nineteenth century, and under the succession of government regimes, the status of religious practice and the political allegiances of the clergy continued to make the cathedral of Notre-Dame a flashpoint for violent confrontation. Catholicism gained ground in France during the Restoration despite the fact that Louis XVIII and his entourage were not ardent followers. The Constitution of June 4, 1814 maintained freedom of religion in France, but declared Catholicism the state religion; both Protestant and Catholic institutions received government funding under its terms. This strengthening of the position of the Catholic church was tempered during the Restoration by anti-clerical sentiments which carried over from the Revolutionary period. Later, the lesser official status accorded to the church under the government of Louis-Philippe was determined early on, in the Constitution of 1830 which demoted Catholicism from state religion to "the religion professed by the majority of the French."

The July Monarchy and Gothic Paris

The association in public opinion between the Catholic church and the deposed monarchs of the Restoration was first evidenced during the "Trois Glorieuses" of July, 1830 when the archbishop's palace, which stood between the south side of Notre-Dame and the Seine, was sacked. According to some newspaper accounts at the time, the crowd forced itself into the palace and found 100 daggers and two barrels of gunpowder secreted away inside. The Catholic newspaper, *L'Ami de la Religion* declared this claim to be "absurd" on the grounds that the monks of the chapter at Notre-Dame were all at least in their seventies, if not their nineties. The paper did recount however, how on the twenty-ninth of July, a mob of men and women numbering between twelve and fifteen hundred, some disguised as monks, burst into the first courtyard of the palace and proceeded to disperse the archives and destroy relics. In the second courtyard, where the archbishop's residence was located, one group descended to the basement and drank up a good amount of the sacramental wine while the rest went upstairs where there ensued "a scene of appalling devastation" as furnishings were broken, burned, or thrown in the river. The Catholic newspaper reported that seven murders had been committed in the course of the pillaging.

The attack on the archbishop's palace was just the most overt expression of a suspicion of Notre-Dame's clergy, and of the archbishop himself, Hyacinthe-Louis de Quélen (1778-1839) who was accused of mixing politics with religion and, in particular, of being skeptical of Louis-Philippe's viability as a ruler. Resentment of de Quélen continued to simmer through the fall of 1830 and into the winter of 1831 when, on February fifteenth, the palace was again attacked. That morning, the trouble started when the interior of the church of St.-Germain-l'Auxerrois was "completely devastated" (according to the police) and the crowd then proceeded to Notre-Dame where they smashed windows with rocks and hurled "the most energetic imprecations against the priests, the Jesuits and the archbishop of Paris." From the cathedral, the crowd moved to the archbishop's apartments (again) where, in the midst of the destruction that ensued, the Seine was filled with the debris of furniture, paintings, hangings, and books. The official account said that the crowd had overrun the National Guard which had been dispatched to protect the palace, but other sources stated that the authorities had stood aside and let the attack take place. In the wake of the event, Prosper Mérimée, the novelist and eventual inspector general of historic monuments during the July Monarchy, wrote to his friend, the novelist Stendhal (the pen name of Marie-Henri Beyle, 1783-

1842) to report that "You missed a pretty spectacle, that of the pillage of the archbishop's palace.[. . .] The National Guard split their sides laughing and didn't stop anything."

After the first attack on the archbishop's palace but before the second, King Louis-Philippe, in December, 1830, resolved to repair it, "as much to make this building functional, as to create employment for the working class." Because the palace had been expanded in 1810 to accommodate a potential residency by the Pope, repairing it and refurnishing it would have been prohibitively expensive. Instead, the prefect of the department of the Seine, Odilon Barrot, recommended demolishing the palace entirely on the grounds that the people of Paris had already provided ample demonstration of their resentment of the archbishop's luxurious accommodations and would balk at spending money to recreate them. What is more significant here is that Barrot also argued for demolishing the palace ruins on aesthetic grounds. He stated that the palace obstructed views of the city's "majestic monument" and blocked improvements to the public ways in its populous quarter. The matter was still unresolved when the second attack took place, but after that, it was impossible even to contemplate restoring the palace. A royal ordonnance of August, 1831 called for the demolition of the building in its entirety. Although the clergy called this "legal violence" (in internal government correspondence) that was being used to reward "popular violence," the remains of the building were eventually razed. In so doing, the administration began the process of isolating Notre-Dame, of making its architecture more visible from the Left Bank. Future restoration projects there would contribute to the opening up of space around Notre-Dame to make this icon of the Gothic style stand unencumbered and accessible to viewers from a number of vantage points.

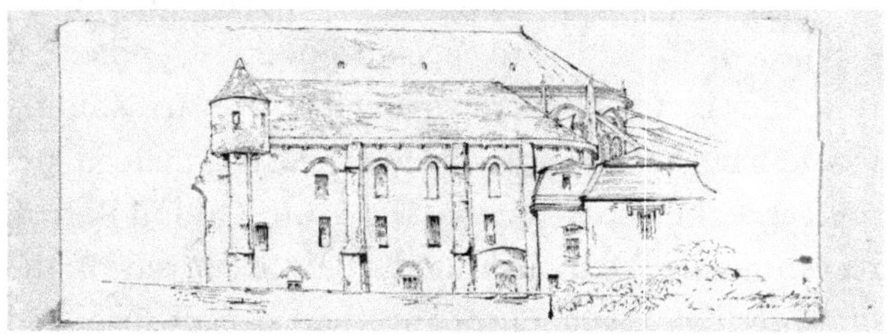

9. Remains of the Archbishop's Palace, Notre Dame, 1831.

Gothic and Neo-Gothic Sculpture at Notre-Dame

The tumultuous political situation in France through the mid-nineteenth century made Notre-Dame a target for destruction, as we have seen, but it also occasioned some enrichment of the decorative program, particularly of the exterior sculpture, around the time of the Revolution of 1848 and in the years that followed. Michael Camille has demonstrated how, as part of their restoration of the cathedral in the 1840s and '50s Viollet-le-Duc and Lassus designed terrifying gargoyles and chimeras

—the latter being figures perched on the balustrades with both animal and human features that do not serve as drain pipes in the way that gargoyles do— that reflected their own conflicted responses to revolutionary violence. An early example of this restored sculpture Camille points out is "Le Rongeur" ("The Devourer") on the cathedral's west façade, designed in 1848-49, around the time of the revolution that brought into being the short-lived Second Republic. This grotesque beast is shown biting the head off an animal whose carcass he clutches in his bony, over-scaled paws which are more like hands.

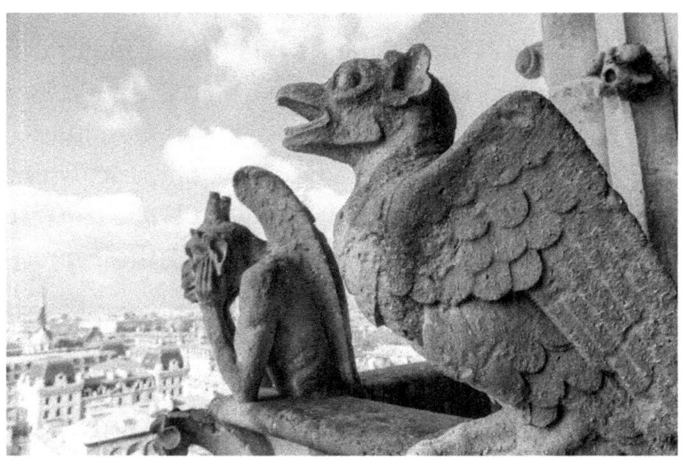

10. Gargoyles of Notre-Dame.

Evidence, perhaps, of Parisians' fears of revolutionary violence, of a return of the Reign of Terror, the mid-century sculpted gargoyles and chimeras were not only tolerated: they eventually became icons of Notre-Dame. Even though they are clearly nineteenth-century additions, some of which have no basis whatsoever in medieval precedent, there has never been (to my knowledge) any move to restore the cathedral's earlier appearance by removing them. Public attachment to the sculptures derives in part from the wide circulation of images of the gargoyles and chimera starting with nineteenth-century paintings, prints, and photographs.

Not so for the signs of Revolutionary destruction. The marks of hammer blows certainly told the story of how Notre-Dame played witness to the major political events of the age. In fact, from the 1840s onward there were critics who worried that the restoration of Notre-Dame would rob the cathedral of the visible traces of France's important, revolutionary history. The Gallery of Kings —without its statues—was considered an eyesore by some, but at least one government official, Antoine Allier (1793–1870), a leftist deputy from the Department of the Hautes-Alpes from 1839 to 1847 who was sculptor himself, thought otherwise. In response to an 1845 funding request for the restoration, he argued against replacing the kings with new figures based on sculptures from other Gothic cathedrals, as was then proposed, and he objected to the very idea of effacing the signs of revolution on Notre-Dame's façade. Allier declared to the Chamber of Deputies: "[E]verything is mystical in the appearance of this gallery: I would not want to change anything about it." The very absence of the kings would represent the moment at which the

Revolution had moved against the material evidence of the crown and church.

Allier's position on the cathedral was an outlier and the replacement of the sculpture went forward. Nonetheless, the question of whether the evidence of destruction, of the Revolution, should remain visible in the fabric of Notre-Dame remained an open one, at least for some observers. For instance, Jules-Antoine Castagnary (1830-88), a progressive art critic, wrote in 1862 (in an article entitled "Notre-Dame Restaurée" published in the *Courrier du Dimanche* on 28 December) that if the restoration of Paris's monuments continued, in a few years the city would have "no more stains on her new clothes." Restoration, Castagnary feared, would mean that the symbolic destruction of the royal and ecclesiastical symbols on Parisian monuments, including Notre-Dame, would have been for naught: "Vainly will history have passed over [the buildings...] Vainly will the Revolution, coming into their sanctuaries like the Angel of Death, have extinguished their candles with its wings and melted their reliquaries with its blazing sword [...]. It would seem that this most recent past must give way to a more ancient past." Castagnary's sympathies were clearly with the revolutionaries, and he regretted the way that restorers tended to emphasize the pre-modern histories of Paris's religious monuments over their connections to more immediate, albeit convulsive, episodes in the nation's history. Castagnary suggests that restoring away the signs of Revolutionary violence was tantamount to suppressing the leftist politics that they represented for him. Writing at the height of the Second Empire, Castagnary confirmed the ongoing importance of Notre-Dame and other Parisian monuments as living representations of the nation's history, even while he lamented the sanitization of that history through restoration.

Chapter 5

The Classicists' Notre-Dame

The Classical View of the Gothic

The last chapter described how the changing political situation in France, between the late eighteenth and mid-nineteenth centuries, had direct consequences for how the physical fabric of the cathedral of Notre-Dame was treated. Politics had an immediate impact on how people saw Notre-Dame because the building carried very specific associations with the church and state. In a parallel way, evolving ideas about medieval architecture, and particularly about the Gothic style and its perceived relationship to classicism (the architecture of ancient Greece and Rome), exerted an important influence on how government and church officials, as well as the architects they employed, dealt with Notre-Dame. The Gothic cathedral of Paris emerged over time from the foundations of earlier sanctuaries on the site; later, classical features were layered over the medieval fabric. They were introductions by architects whose sympathies lay with classicism, rather than with the Gothic style of the cathedral. And when the first attempts were made to restore the cathedral, under the empire of Napoléon I —mostly to get rid of evidence of the French Revolution— they were carried out by architects who similarly lacked much feeling for the cathedral's style.

Vasari's "Gothic"

That style, the Gothic, was melded with imported elements in French architecture of the fifteenth and sixteenth centuries to form a particularly French Renaissance idiom. At the same time, the Gothic —as a particular aesthetic mode— was codified by the first art historians. The invention of a concept of the Gothic as a period architectural style of the Middle Ages is often attributed to the "father of art history," the multi-talented Italian Giorgio Vasari (1511-1574) whose *Le Vite de' più eccellenti pittori, scultori, e architettori*, or *The Lives of the Most Excellent Painters, Sculptors, and Architects*, was published in two editions, in 1550 and

1568. A painter, architect, and historian, as well as an author, Vasari wrote, in his *Lives*, the biographies of some of the greatest practitioners of his time, thereby creating the original canon of Renaissance artists. The narrative arc of Vasari's *Lives*, writes Anne-Marie Sankovitch (in "The Myth of the 'Myth of the Medieval,'" *Res* 40 [Autumn 2001]: 29-50) begins with a moment of purported perfection in the classical art and architecture of antiquity, descends into a "period of death and ruin, of pure anticlassicism," during the Middle Ages, then culminates triumphantly with the "rebirth" of classicism during the Renaissance. In a passage added to the 1568 edition of the *Lives*, Vasari fulminates about what he considers the depravity of the Gothic, or as he calls it, the "maniera tedescchi," or literally, the "German manner."

After having described the classical architectural orders (Rustic, Doric, Ionic, Corinthian, and Composite) in the *Lives*, Vasari concludes that, "There is another type of works called *tedeschi,* which in their ornaments and proportions are very different from the antique and the modern. Today they are not used by the most gifted architects, who instead flee from them as monstrous and barbarous and forsaken of all that comprises order [...]." Vasari cringed at Gothic portals with "columns that are thin and twisted like vines and do not have the strength to bear a load," or facades with "a malediction of little tabernacles" and "so many pyramids and points and leaves that it appears impossible that they can stand up or even bear their own weight." The author then points directly to the originators of this maligned style: "This *maniera* was invented by the Goths" who made "buildings in this *maniera*: they turned the vaults with pointed segments, and filled all of Italy with this malediction of buildings" (Sankovitch trans.). Vasari's association of the style of the late Middle Ages with the Goths led to the term "Gothic" being applied to the architecture of the period regardless of where in Europe or Great Britain it was constructed and by whom.

Where later French critics parted company with Vasari was with his description of Gothic structure, or rather, his relative inattention to it. Discussing the tabernacles he abhorred, Vasari wrote that "they seem to have been made of paper rather than of stone and marble." True, from their interiors, the walls of a Rayonnant church or cathedral seemed paper thin, but they were, a French critic might have observed, supported by a structure that was carefully and precisely calculated. The French prided themselves on the sophistication, even the daring, of their stone constructions, most notably, the monuments of the Gothic style in the Île-de-France. While classicism would provide the foundation for French architecture from the Renaissance well into the nineteenth century and arguably beyond it, the Gothic was never entirely lost sight of. In fact, a "Graeco-Gothic tradition" (to use architectural historian Robin Middleton's phrase) was threaded through French architectural thought from the Renaissance into the nineteenth century: it promoted the lightness and structural clarity of the Gothic at the same time that it championed the use of classical forms.

In France, in contrast to other European nations and Great Britain, there were powerful government institutions that supported —and in some times and contexts, demanded— the use of classical architecture. The most important of these were the French Academy and the École des Beaux-arts (School of Fine Arts) that operated under its aegis in Paris. From its founding in the seventeenth century through the early twentieth century, the École des Beaux-arts remained the most prestigious art and architecture school in France and drew students from throughout the country and abroad. The curriculum heavily emphasized the mastery of the classical tradition and for budding architects, the acquisition of skills in the "composition" of buildings using the principles of symmetry, axiality, and the accommodation of a building's plan within a simple, geometric figure. Architecture students also learned drawing skills, especially as apprentices in the workshops, or "ateliers," of practicing architects, which they put to use in the competitions which marked their progress through the École's curriculum. The culmination of this educational process was the "Prix de Rome," or Rome Prize competition in which the winner received a fellowship that enabled him to spend a period of four or five years at the French Academy in Rome, studying ancient monuments.

The most successful of students at the École des Beaux-arts would go on to careers in government service. In contrast to other countries, in France the most prestigious positions for an architect were in the architectural agencies of the national government, of which the Service des Edifices diocésains (Service of Diocesan Buildings), founded in 1816, was one. Important Gothic buildings, like Notre-Dame, occupied complex positions in the government architectural services since they were considered to possess both utility for the practice of religion and significance from a purely architectural, secular point of view. At many points in the post-Revolutionary period, secular and religious authorities came into conflict about whether religious function trumped architectural significance, or vice versa, in the churches and cathedrals of the Middle Ages. This tension, as well as the struggles that emerged when classically-trained architects tried to adapt the Gothic building to new tastes and uses, characterized Notre-Dame's history from the sixteenth to the nineteenth century. Both secular and religious authorities exerted their influences over the restoration of the cathedral.

Classical Notre-Dame

While the French Renaissance had a minimal impact on Notre-Dame, a period of transformation began in 1699 when King Louis XIV (reigned 1643 to 1715) undertook some projects for the cathedral that had been planned by his predecessor, Louis XIII, and published in 1638. The Gothic altar was replaced by a modern counterpart and the fourteenth-century choir stalls were removed. They were replaced (between 1710 and 1715) by the current choir stalls which have simple seats surmounted by elaborately-carved wood plaques to the design of architect Robert de Cotte (1656-1735). In the same period, marble plaques were installed around the columns, including at the apse where Gothic arcades were replaced by large Doric columns clad in red and white marble supporting semi-circular arches. These alterations masked the Gothic character of Notre-Dame with architectural elements based on classical forms and evidenced a lack of interest in medieval architecture which was characteristic of the period. Or worse: the construction at Notre-Dame betrayed a absence of sympathy for the Gothic which prevailed among many critics in the centuries after Vasari and others had begun to speak of it as "barbaric."

Louis XV's long reign, which lasted from 1715 to 1774, brought about the "grattage" ("scraping") and whitewashing of the interior walls of the cathedral, as well as the installation of iron balustrades at the galleries of the nave, crossing, and choir, as government records document. Between 1741 and 1753, clear glass was installed in place of many stained glass windows (notably excepting the large rose windows at the north and south transepts, and at the west façade), and during the third quarter of the eighteenth century, blue pavement replaced tomb slabs on the floor. Neoclassical architect Jacques-Germain Soufflot (1713-80), who is most well known for the design of the church of Sainte-Geneviève (later to become the Panthéon) on the Montaigne Sainte-Geneviève, demolished the original sacristy at Notre-Dame (which separated the two courtyards of the archbishop's palace) and the Gothic gallery that led to it. He replaced them (starting in 1756) with the sacristy which was still partially standing by the early 1840s, despite the attacks of 1830-31. The comprehensive restoration of the cathedral that started in the 1840s included the removal of the old sacristy's remains and its eventual replacement by a new one designed by Lassus and Viollet-le-Duc. The restoration also removed Soufflot's alterations to the central portal on the west facade, according to Jean-Marie Pérouse de Montclos (in his article, "Soufflot autour de Notre-Dame," in the volume *Autour de Notre-Dame* [2003]). There, in 1771 Soufflot had removed the central column that divided the portal, in order to accommodate official processions, and then installed a pointed arch above the doors that extended into the original tympanum.

A short time later, on the exterior of the cathedral, beginning in 1773, the architect Boulland removed all decoration from the chapels on the south side of the nave and installed a blank wall in that location, terminating in crenellation. Several years later, the flying buttresses were encased in heavy masonry, which far from having the desired effect of protecting them, hastened their decay. Further destruction took place just prior to the Revolution, in 1787, when the architect Parvy was charged with the restoration of the façade and in carrying out that project removed any masonry items that were difficult to repair, including gargoyles and column capitals. Although the Revolution would soon lead to some deliberate destruction of the cathedral, in fact, alterations motivated by a desire to minimize the Gothic flavor of the interior, or clumsy repairs to the exterior, had already begun the process of deterioration.

Napoléon and Notre-Dame

As many historians have observed, the French Revolution brought about a deliberate and self-conscious break with the *ancien régime* —even a new calendar was adopted. The Revolution thus could only be understood as a rupture with the preceding history and it was one with which French historians had to contend in the following decades. The establishment of the first Napoleonic Empire was one attempt to bridge the chasm of the Revolution by a variety of means, but most importantly for Notre-Dame, by reestablishing the Catholic church in France and making reference in works of art and architecture to the Roman Empire.

We have already observed how Napoléon created a maintenance fund for Notre-Dame and brought back a chapter of monks to the cathedral. Moreover, the Emperor sought to restore the building's exterior to its original splendor, as the antiquarian A.P.M. announced in his monograph, *Description Historique de la Basilique Métopolitaine de Paris, et des Curiosités de son Trésor* (*Historical Description of the Metropolitan Basilica of Paris, and of the Curiosities of its Treasury*, 1811). Gilbert predicted that the "devastations" of the chapels around the choir would disappear (presumably, meaning that the new materials, columns, and arches would be removed) and the "total exterior restoration" of the cathedral would follow. That meant repairing the destruction that had taken place during the Revolution, including replacing the kings in the gallery above the portals on the west façade. Gilbert suggested adding to them an image of the "hero" who had brought religious practice back to Notre-Dame —Emperor Napoléon I— to "conserve for future races the memory of his munificence with respect to this church." This proposal meant rewriting the history of France as it was inscribed on the monument itself, effacing the traces of the Revolution and substituting for them a memorial to Napoléon who, in May, 1809, had annexed the Papal States to the Empire and imprisoned the Pope.

Although this moment signaled a new respect for Notre-Dame, there was not yet a government architect available to carry out the work with a corresponding feeling for the historic building. Enter Étienne-Hippolyte Godde (1781-1869) who had risen through the government architectural services to the position of "chief designer" under the architect Alexandre-Théodore Brongniart (1739-1813). Brongniart was the author of some important neoclassical works, including the Paris Bourse (1808), the stock exchange building that is notable for being totally encircled on its exterior by Corinthian columns in the manner of a classical temple. Although Brongniart was the titular director of the Notre-Dame restoration after 1810, he accomplished little before his death three years later.

Godde was just as much a classicist at Brongniart, having been a student at the École des Beaux-arts, although not an especially successful one. After a number of failures in the Prix de Rome competition, he entered the architectural service of the Department of the Seine (basically contiguous with the city of Paris) in 1801. After Brongniart's death, Godde held a virtual monopoly on ecclesiastical buildings in Paris, some of which he restored or simply maintained. He also built at least five new churches between 1813 and 1830. In the early July Monarchy, Godde was edged out of practice, and came under increasing criticism for his "regrettable mutilation" of the towers of St.-Germain-des-Prés (as a modern biographer, Marie-Christine Ferrand de la Conté-Gélis put it in her 1980 thesis on Godde at the École Nationale des Chartes) and his "restoration" of the apse at the Abbey of Corbie of which one vault had collapsed, killing a half-dozen workers.

The Bourbon Restoration and Notre-Dame

Brongniart's ambitious restoration project at Notre-Dame began in 1812 at the north side of the nave, between the façade tower and the transept. His death, and the fall of the Empire the following year, brought the project to a halt. Once again, the decorative program of Notre-Dame had to be changed to reflect a new political regime. All imperial symbols —including "N"s, crowns, and gilt bees— were ordered taken off the building and its furnishings. The Archbishop of Paris requested in October, 1814 that the monogram of the Virgin Mary replace the "N"s and that the fleur-de-lys, the symbol of the restored Bourbon monarchy, take the place of bees. During the Restoration, additional changes to the decorative treatment of Notre-Dame were proposed to represent a continuity with the earlier Bourbon monarchs. For instance, proposals were made for sculptures of Louis XIII and Louis XIV to be placed in the sanctuary, and bronze fleurs-de-lys installed along the borders of the windows.

One of the voices raised in opposition to the treatment of the cathedral during the Bourbon Restoration belonged to Jean-Marie Bertrand de Vienne, one of the monks at Notre-Dame, who appealed to the government in 1817 for an appointment as "conservator" of the cathedral, in which capacity he proposed to keep a watchful eye on the work there. In specific, he asked for permission to oppose the capricious actions of architects who seemed to "depart more and more from the general plan of the building, and to substitute for it everywhere modern constructions, that don't go with the whole."

In 1818, de Vienne's criticisms were echoed by the architect François Debret (1777-1850), whose own restoration of St.-Denis, also came under fire. He argued in a document sent to the Ministry of the Interior that while considerable sums had been spent on Notre-Dame "to efface the ruins of vandalism and to restore to it its ancient luster," little had been achieved. Indeed, in 1820, Godde was still working on the north side of the nave, repairing sculpture and masonry through means that would become controversial. In specific, loose stones were being re-adhered to the walls with a kind of adhesive or mastic. Little progress was made before work halted in 1822, not to be returned to until 1837. While observers and critics tended to agree that not much had been done to make Notre-Dame look better during the Empire and Restoration, that was not for lack of funding. A later report by the government's director of the Catholic church to the minister of the interior, dated July 1842, reckoned that under Brongniart and Goode about a half million francs had been spent on the restoration.

Napoléon understood, just as did the Revolutionary governments, that France's medieval churches and cathedrals were symbolically important enough that they had to be laid claim to. For the Revolution that meant, at least at first, their destruction. For the Emperor, achieving symbolic ownership of medieval religious buildings meant restoring them, especially Notre-Dame whose importance to the city of Paris and as a "national" monument (as de Vienne and other more influential spokespeople agreed), was a means of connecting with institutions of secular and religious authority from the *ancien régime*. The problem was that architectural theory and education in France, which continued to privilege the classical tradition, had not yet caught up with a major conceptual shift in sentiments about the architecture of the Middle Ages.

That sea change in the conception of the medieval monument, which took place during the first several decades of the nineteenth century, was this: the churches and cathedrals of the Middle Ages were no longer seen as buildings that should evolve over the course of time in response to changing needs; rather, they should be locked in the past, in a state that approximated their "original" conditions. However, two caveats are needed here. First, not everyone bought into this new idea of the medieval religious building. For instance, religious authorities often sought to make changes to churches and other religious buildings as their needs and practices changed. Second, as the building history of Notre-Dame makes abundantly clear, it was very hard to say just what the "original" appearance of a Gothic church or cathedral actually was, given that structures often emerged, over the course of long periods of time, from the foundations of earlier buildings and as reflections of successions of architects and patrons. That is, there often *was no* original building to recreate.

During the first several decades of the nineteenth century, archaeological and historical interest in medieval architecture increased and provided the basis for the eventual restorations of Gothic churches and cathedrals. However, as we saw in the previous chapter, the political allegiances of the clergy during the July Monarchy precluded government investment in their buildings, specifically in Notre-Dame, during the 1830s. That produced a hiatus in repairs to the building. The extent and character of those projected restorations were still being based on Brongniart's 1811 proposal and were increasingly considered stylistically outmoded by some government administrators.

Notre-Dame, the Catholic Revival, and the Early Gothic Revival

The 1820s and '30s saw little work accomplished at Notre-Dame despite the fact, pointed out by a number of government reports, that a substantial amount of money was spent on the project. During the work-stoppage, a religious movement, based at Notre-Dame, nonetheless gained momentum and lent support to later preservation efforts. It coincided historically with growing interest in medieval architecture, spurred by the publication of Victor Hugo's 1831 novel *Notre-Dame de Paris* and by the Romantic movement more generally.

Liberal Catholicism at Notre-Dame

The restoration of Notre-Dame was more energetically promoted by the government when the cathedral became the site of a new liberal Catholic movement which sought to disassociate the church from any particular political regime. At the center of the movement was Félicité de Lamennais (1782-1854). He had already co-authored two books about the Catholic church with his older brother Jean-Marie before becoming a priest in 1816. After that time, Félicité continued to write on religious themes, including an 1829 pamphlet on the Revolution's opposition to the church in which he reaffirmed the ideal of a society where religious belief would be a unifying force rather than a source of division. With his collaborators Charles de Montalembert (1810-70) and Henri Lacordaire (1802-64, a priest), de Lamennais founded a journal called *L'Avenir* (*The Future*) published in 1830-31. It called for "the total separation of church and state," freedom of the press and education from state control, and the end to centralization which was prevalent in the French government administration. De Lamennais advocated, instead, for state and local self-determination and even for the government to respect the authority of the "père de famille" (male head of household).

Lacordaire propounded the viewpoints of *L'Avenir* (set out in the journal's Dec. 7, 1830 issue) at Notre-Dame starting in 1835 at the instigation of a group of Catholic students who pressed for his appointment there. The archbishop de Quélen was wary of Lacordaire's attempt to generate a religious revival outside of political boundaries but he acquiesced. De Montalembert's description of Lacordaire's presence at Notre-Dame in 1835 was quoted by Paul Thureau-Dangin in his book *L'Église et l'État sous la Monarchie de Juillet* (1880): "[...] the old basilica of Notre-Dame was filled with an immense and unfamiliar crowd. Below its vaults that had been deserted for so long and where the solitude had been rarely interrupted, over the course of a half century, except by official ceremonies during the Empire and the Restoration or by the profanations of revolutionary impiety, six thousand men, for the most part young, representing the entirety of intellectual life in the period and all the hopes for the future, pressed to hear the words of a priest." Despite such a resounding success, de Quélen curtailed Lacordaire's preaching at Notre-Dame in 1836, in response to the opposition to the new liberal ideas that came from the older clergy. Lacordaire's place at Notre-Dame was assumed by the less controversial Père de Ravignan who continued to draw a large crowd.

The deteriorated condition of the cathedral itself became all the more obvious as its use intensified. In 1842 de Montalembert reported to a government agency that the crowd assembled for one of de Ravignan's recent sermons had noticed the "deplorable state of abandon and uncleanliness" which then characterized the cathedral. A small amount of money was raised from the faithful to pay for improvements, but it could hardly put a dent in the deferred maintenance, let alone underwrite the full-blown restoration that was then being contemplated. That work would be guided principally by secular architectural interests, rather than by considerations of how well the cathedral functioned as a place of worship.

The body that was able to help spearhead the project was the Commission des Monuments Historiques (Commission of Historic Monuments), founded early in the July Monarchy. Soon, it was headed by Prosper Mérimée who, as Inspector General of Historic Monuments ushered in a new era in historic preservation in France, working side-by-side with Viollet-le-Duc. The two established the government architectural service that undertook ambitious restorations of many of France's most canonical Gothic monuments from the July Monarchy through the Second Empire. They built on the growing body of archaeological and antiquarian knowledge of the nation's historic buildings to create a cadre of trusted administrators and architects who were passionate about the Gothic and who increasingly replaced their older, classicist counterparts. Mérimée supported Viollet-le-Duc's work from the time that the architect was a very young man and he would go on to restore many important buildings. But none, perhaps, was as visible as Notre-Dame and certainly none was believed to belong so firmly to the nation as a whole.

Chapter 6

Notre-Dame and the Medieval School

Viollet-le-Duc, Jean-Baptiste Lassus and the Cathedral of Paris

As a young child, Viollet-le-Duc reported later in life, he had a formative, although traumatic experience, in Notre-Dame. In his *Entretiens sur l'architecture* (*Lectures on Architecture*, 1863-72), he recounted how one day, while "entrusted to the care of an old servant," he was carried into the cathedral where there was a funeral of some kind taking place, since the building was draped in black:

> "My gaze rested on the painted glass of the southern rose-window, through which the rays of sun were streaming, colored with the most brilliant hues. I still see the place where our progress was interrupted by the crowd. All at once the roll of the great organ was heard; but for me, the sound was the singing of the rose window before me. In vain did my old guide attempt to deter me; the impression became more and more vivid, until my imagination led me to believe that such panes of glass emitted grave and solemn sounds, while others produced shriller and more piercing tones, so that at last my terror became so intense that he was obliged to take me out."

In his definitive 2014 biography of the architect (*Architecture and the Historical Imagination: Eugène-Emmanuel Viollet-le-Duc, 1814-1879*), Martin Bressani considers this episode as crucial to Viollet-le-Duc's entire life, which was largely devoted to the study and restoration of medieval, especially Gothic, monuments. In this hallucinatory experience, the Gothic building literally comes alive for the future architect. Much later, Viollet-le-Duc would take a central role in reviving Notre-Dame as a place of worship, but more importantly in his mind, as an image of the Gothic period and as a testament to French architectural genius. In the early 1840s,

Viollet-le-Duc and his collaborator, Jean-Baptiste Lassus, won the important position of restoration architects for Notre-Dame through a competition, a departure from the usual way in which architects were awarded such commissions, which was by appointment. The opening of a limited competition, which provided an opportunity to consider various approaches to the project, reflected the general dissatisfaction with the work that had been carried out —or that had failed to be carried out— on the cathedral over the course of the previous two decades. In every way, this was a defining moment for the cathedral of Notre-Dame. It was the point at which centuries of deterioration were reversed, the building was stabilized structurally, and it gained what was —until the fire of April 15, 2019— the form that modern viewers are familiar with. This transformation came about as a result of the "Medieval" or "Archaeological" school of architects and administrators.

The definitive nineteenth-century form the cathedral took was based on the physical evidence of the building itself, but also on Viollet-le-Duc's, and to some extent Lassus's, vision of what a Gothic cathedral should be, regardless of what it might actually have looked like when it was completed. In the eighth volume of his *Dictionnaire Raisonné de l'Architecture Française, du XIe au XVIe Siècle* (*Dictionary of French Architecture, from the XIth to the XVIth Centuries* [1854-68]), in the entry on "Restoration," Viollet-le-

Duc announced his point of view: "Both the word and the thing are modern. To restore an edifice means neither to maintain it, nor to repair it, nor to rebuild it; it means to reestablish it in a finished state which may in fact have never actually existed at any given time" (Kenneth D. Whitehead, trans.). This bold statement acknowledged what was certainly the case for Notre-Dame, namely, that it would be nearly impossible to say at what point it had actually been "finished," given that it had emerged incrementally over time. Viollet-le-Duc also claimed authority here, at least implicitly, for conceiving and giving form to a vision of an historic building in its imagined completeness through the process of restoration. This concept thoroughly permeated the restoration of Notre-Dame from the 1840s through the 1860s.

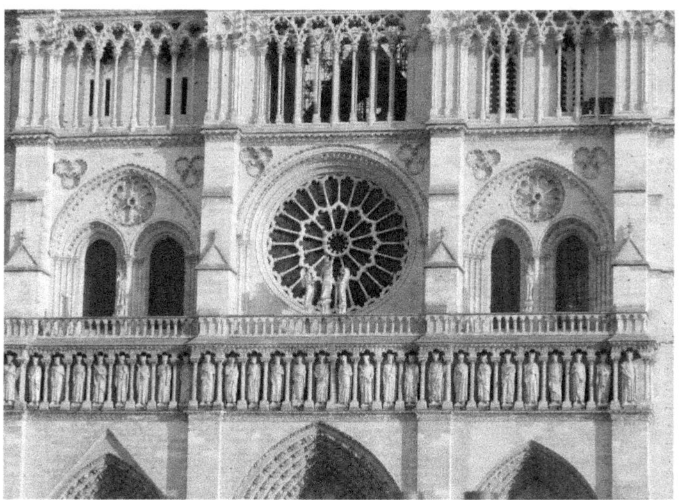

11. West Façade of Notre-Dame, Rose Window and Gallery of Kings.

Viollet-le-Duc's path to the architectural profession differed from those of his neoclassical predecessors at Notre-Dame. He did not attend the École des Beaux-arts but instead studied with two architects in Paris and travelled independently to Italy in 1836-37. When he returned to France, he drew medieval buildings for the important publication edited by the Baron Isidore Taylor, the multi-volume *Voyages Pittoresques et Romantiques dans l'Ancienne France* (*Picturesque and Romantic Travels in Old France* [1820-78]). Then he obtained government architectural posts, through family connections and with the support of Mérimée. Viollet-le-Duc came out of an artistic and intellectual *milieu*, rather than a religious one, and his view of the Gothic was correspondingly secular. Hence, his restoration projects would emphasize structural and historical concerns, rather than address the space needs of the clergy. In fact, in his first independent restoration project, of the Romanesque church of the Madeleine at Vézelay in Burgundy, beginning in 1840, he attempted to remove religious practice from the main sanctuary as much as possible and to carry out a reconstruction that clarified the building's structure and showed it to be an important precursor to the later Gothic style.

The restoration of Notre-Dame was built upon Viollet-le-Duc's earlier experience, and that of his collaborator, Lassus. Their joint submission to the competition was born from their work together on the restoration of the Sainte-Chappelle in 1840. While the two men had different backgrounds —Lassus had trained at the École des Beaux-arts although he was critical of the institution— they shared a passion for medieval architecture. As his major biographer, Jean-Michel Leniaud, noted (in *Jean-Baptiste Lassus [1807-1857] ou Le Temps Retrouvé des Cathédrales* [1980]), Lassus received encouragement for his study of medieval architecture from his teacher and mentor, Henri Labrouste, an influential mid-century practitioner. The respectful tone of the restoration proposal Viollet-le-Duc and Lassus submitted for Notre-Dame has sometimes been credited to the influence of the latter architect. However, the choice to sound a cautious note in the proposal was also strategic at a time when there was a great deal of suspicion about where the money already spent on Notre-Dame had disappeared to, and about the capabilities of the architects who had worked on the project previously.

In July, 1842 Godde's work on Notre-Dame came in for particular criticism. His use of adhesives and patches to repair the masonry was said, by a government commission appointed to evaluate the work, to have destroyed the "grave and imposing character" of the monument, and to have left the restored sculpture "lifeless." That summer, the director of the Catholic division of the government administration, Pierre Dessauret (1794-1869), concluded that Godde lacked the proper feeling for and knowledge of the Gothic, which had been demonstrated by the "strangest errors" he made at Notre-Dame and elsewhere. Significantly, at this point, Dessauret capitulated to the press, literary figures, and archaeologists who had pressed for "a complete restoration" of Notre-Dame, not just piecemeal fixes. He imagined (in a report to the Minister of Justice and Cults, Martin du Nord, dated July 1842 and preserved in the Archives nationales) a massive project that would put the cathedral back in its "normal" state and rid the interior of the "parasite decorations" that had been added since the turn of the eighteenth century. Those included the classical columns and arches in the choir and Soufflot's additions, the clear glass in the windows, and the whitewash on the walls. Not only was the project to be "great and national," it was also supposed to serve as a model for other cities and localities contemplating the restoration of their own historic monuments. The summer of 1842 was a watershed moment: at that point, government officials started to talk about a comprehensive restoration of Notre-Dame —something that had not been proposed previously— and to argue that it had to be directed by an architect (or architects) with specialized knowledge of medieval architecture.

The Notre-Dame Competition

The idea of a limited competition for the project came about only gradually as several architects were called upon to submit proposals for a total restoration of

Notre-Dame which would return it, as Dessauret said, to its "primitive physiognomy." He called upon Viollet-le-Duc and Lassus to enter the competition on the basis of the work they had already carried out in Paris which had been well regarded. Given the haphazard way in which the competition had come about, it is not surprising that the three contestants (with one of them being the Viollet-le-Duc/Lassus team) had been given virtually no direction in the preparation of their proposals, nor had they been provided with a budget, although by early 1843 that was set at two million francs. Among the parts of the project which were emphasized by the Conseil des Bâtiments civils (Civil Buildings Council) was the "restoration of the central portal in its original state," the replacement of lost portal sculpture, and the repopulation of the Gallery of Kings. Getting rid of the "traces of mutilation" that dated to the Revolutionary period were a high priority, as they were felt to be "obvious" and even "shocking." Both the Catholic and secular branches of the national government were consulted about the proposals for the restoration submitted in 1843 and all were found to have certain strengths and shortcomings. The evaluation of the three proposals continued into 1844 and while, according to the Conseil des Bâtiments civils, two had basic conceptual and structural defects, Viollet-le-Duc's and Lassus's project had only minor faults in the detailing that could be corrected.

Defining Restoration

The year 1844 was another key moment for the French architectural administration's formulation of what could be considered a modern concept of restoration, and they identified the project for Notre-Dame's renewal by Viollet-le-Duc and Lassus as being consistent with it. In its deliberations of March 11, 1844 (preserved in the Archives nationales), the Conseil des Bâtiments civils affirmed that: "By the word restoration, it must be repeated again, *we mean above all the conservation of what exists, the reproduction of what manifestly existed*" [emphasis theirs]. Succinctly, this statement articulated an evidenced-based concept of restoration. (It was not quite the definition Viollet-le-Duc would offer later in his *Dictionnaire*.)

This objective of taking an historic church, or in this case a cathedral, back to its documented appearance came into conflict with the religious uses of such buildings, as architect and author César Daly remarked in the *Revue Générale de l'Architecture et des Travaux Publics* (1843). In the debate over the Notre-Dame restoration, Daly found "another example of the deplorable conflict that today exists relative to the sacred buildings erected in the Middle Ages. Some see in them historic monuments, the work of our fathers, the eloquent testimony of centuries past; others, by way of contrast, insensitive to the poetry of memory, only want to see there a building dedicated to religion and its needs." Daly favored the project by Viollet-le-Duc and Lassus, but he doubted they could tread the fine line they described in their proposal between returning the cathedral to its "splendor," on the one hand, and to operating by strict, archaeological principles, on the other. In their published proposal for the restoration of Notre-Dame, the architects dared to imagine a project that would resolve the contradiction Daly identified: through their work, the architects insisted, "richness" would grow out of "prudent restorations."

In the summer of 1845 Viollet-le-Duc's and Lassus's project received special funding from the federal government, to the tune of more than 2.5 million francs for both the renovation of the cathedral itself and the construction of a new sacristy. In the work that was carried out, historians have argued, Lassus was the careful archaeologist and Viollet-le-Duc the more liberal interpreter of the historical record, whose efforts after his collaborator's death in 1857 departed radically from the very cautious proposals of 1843.

Despite the official support for the original proposal, the funds voted for it were nothing like enough to actually carry it out, since the architects' estimate was more than five million francs. So, Viollet-le-Duc and Lassus revised their proposal to include only necessary repairs to Notre-Dame and to put off any work that was "pure decoration." Thus, in 1845 the Conseil des Bâtiments civils included five categories of work to be carried out. First, the flying buttresses, roofs, and terraces of the chapels and aisles were to be restored, the gutters repaired, and the gargoyles replaced. Second, the west façade was to be restored, which included the removal of Soufflot's central portal and the replacement of statues in the Gallery of Kings. Third, the two transept gables were to be consolidated and the rose window at the north side restored. Fourth, the flying buttresses and roofs of the nave chapels were to be rebuilt. And fifth, the nave, choir, and tribune vaults were to be restored. This proposal was breathtaking in its breadth and despite claims to the contrary, it included some "pure decoration," including gargoyles and sculpted figures. But those were so important to the imagery of Notre-Dame, in the first case, and to the erasure of the traces of the Revolution in the second, that they were included anyway.

The Definitive Restoration of Notre-Dame

Sculpture contracts were executed by 1847 but the worksite was shut down by mid-April, 1850 when the funds were exhausted. A member of the clergy, named Lhuez, described the project in June, 1850 to a government administrator in a letter preserved in the Archives nationales. He alluded to "A [new] sacristy in white stone butted up against a façade black in color, a portal covered in beams and scaffolding, vaults uncovered that let water into the church, chapels nude and ignoble, that's the Cathedral of Paris!" As Lhuez observed, the sacristy's masonry walls and iron roof structure were complete, although work on the new building continued until it was blessed by the archbishop of Paris, Mgr. Sibour on April 15, 1854. Jean-Pierre Cartier and Odile Pinard (in *Notre-Dame de Paris* [2012-19]) note that the team of craftspeople who would later work on the cathedral began with the sacristy which was intended to harmonize with the thirteenth-century fabric of the cathedral.

More or less rectangular in plan, the sacristy joins the side of the cathedral with a courtyard that has corridors at the east and west sides that lead to the cathedral. The ground floor of the building contains five rooms that served as the sacristy and treasury. On the floor above, an apartment was provided for the vicar who was in charge of the sacristy. Since it served as a vestry for the clergy, the sacristy was fitted out with cupboards for the priests' vestments. But, however much the sacristy served practical functions in support of the religious use of the cathedral, Viollet-le-Duc and Lassus did not ignore its decoration. On the exterior, sculpted figures represented the saints of Paris, including Saint Louis and Saint Denis. Some of these figures also appeared in the extensive stained glass of the sacristy, which was not completed until 1867.

The reconstruction of the sacristy was required by the virtual destruction of the previous building, designed by Soufflot, during the Revolution and in the attacks of 1830 and 1831. The contents of the treasury were also dispersed on those occasions. Élisabeth Pauly (in *Notre-Dame de Paris*, 2012-19) recounts that during the Revolutionary period, on March 3, 1791, all objects in the treasury not considered essential to religious practice were confiscated by the state; on September 10, 1792 the remaining objects of value were taken from the treasury which was pillaged just over thirty years later —twice. Nonetheless, the treasury of Notre-Dame later acquired important relics. Most significant were those for which Saint Louis had built the Sainte-Chapelle: the Crown of Thorns and a reputed piece of the True Cross on which Christ was crucified. Those two relics were spared in 1794 when the other sacred objects from the Sainte-Chapelle were sent to the mint to be melted down. Later, the two gems of the Saint-Chapelle's collection of relics were transferred to Notre-Dame. Part of Viollet-le-Duc's work on the sacristy was the design of a new reliquary for the Crown of Thorns; he also designed an elaborate reliquary (produced in 1857) for other relics, those associated with Saint Louis himself (including a linen tunic worn by him) which had been given to Notre-Dame in 1804.

Many of the furnishings of treasury designed by Viollet-le-Duc were only completed well after the Sacristy itself was structurally complete, around

1850. At that point, when work on the cathedral stopped due to lack of funds, Viollet-le-Duc defended his and Lassus's efforts at Notre-Dame, arguing that the reasons for the cost overruns were the discovery of a greater degree of masonry deterioration than previously thought, and the slipshod repairs made by their predecessors. What is perhaps most significant in his account, contained in a report on what had been accomplished as of December 15, 1850 (conserved in the Archives nationales), was Viollet-le-Duc's statement that the flying buttresses around the choir had been so deteriorated that they could only be repaired by taking them down and rebuilding them. He anticipated doing the same for the nave buttresses. Still to be carried out were the sculpture restoration at the façade and the repairs to masonry and rose windows at the transepts.

Progress continued to be stalled by financial issues and political events. A funding bill requesting nearly six million francs was sent to the National Assembly in 1851, but its passage was interrupted by political events that eventuated in the coup d'état of Napoléon III on December second of that year. Shortly thereafter, on January 1, 1852, the coup was celebrated in a religious service, a *Te Deum*, held at Notre-Dame. In her biography of Viollet-le-Duc, Françoise Bercé has described the elaborate temporary décor that the architect, in collaboration with Lassus, devised for the occasion. There were bunting and banners on the west façade, as well as throughout the interior, which was illuminated by 13,000 candles. Also on the façade, the great rose window was stretched with a blue cloth decorated with gold stars. This temporary enhancement of the cathedral, as well as its use for such an important event, could only have generated enthusiasm for its eventual full-scale restoration.

The clergy pushed for the project through 1852 and 1853 on the grounds that Notre-Dame was important not only to the faithful of Paris, but to all of France. This argument took some time to gain enough support that the work could begin again, which it did in 1854. At that point, the restoration of sculpture at the façade was undertaken: it included the Sainte-Anne portal at the south and the Portal of the Virgin at the north. As was mentioned previously, the Sainte-Anne portal contains elements dating to the twelfth century; some related elements are in the collections of the Metropolitan Museum of Art in New York and in the Musée National du Moyen Âge —Thermes et Hôtel de Cluny, Paris. The prominent central motif of the tympanum is the Virgin in Majesty and she is complemented elsewhere on the portal by scenes from the life of the Virgin and the infancy of Christ, among other subjects. To either side of the door are four jamb figures, restorations based on a 1725 printed image of the originals.

The Portal of the Virgin, which is thought to have been realized in the 1210s, lost its sculpture during the Revolution and was restored in the nineteenth century under the direction of Viollet-le-Duc who recommended the use of a model drawn from Amiens cathedral for the trumeau figures of the Virgin and Child. The focal point of the tympanum is the coronation of the Virgin. Noteworthy among the nineteenth-century jamb figures on the left side of the portal is that of Saint Denis who is shown holding his own decapitated head.

At the central portal, where Soufflot had changed the tympanum to accommodate processions, and where twelve jamb figures of the Apostles were removed in 1793, restoration began in 1853 and was completed in 1856. Soufflot had removed the trumeau between the two doors and had also broken through the center portions of the two lintels, the horizontal elements above the door openings, while keeping their ends in place. Viollet-le-Duc had the original ends of the lower lintel removed and a replacement made, using an eighteenth-century print as evidence of what the portal had looked like prior to Soufflot's intervention. A new trumeau figure of Christ was produced in 1855 by the sculptor Adolphe Victor Geoffroy-Dechaume (1816-93) with whom Viollet-le-Duc worked closely for fifteen years.

The all-important Gallery of Kings was restored beginning in the mid-1850s, a decade or so after Viollet-le-Duc and Lassus penned their initial proposal, as Bernard Fonquernie has observed in his comprehensive study of these sculptures (in the *Bulletin Monumental*, tome 157, n°4 [1999]: 347-354). This project was part of the extensive work carried out by Geoffroy-Dechaume, in this case with the assistance of his colleague Chenillion. Both men were portraitists, so it is perhaps not surprising the one of the kings bore a resemblance to Viollet-le-Duc himself. The insertion of sculpted figures in the gallery removed one of the more shocking examples of Revolutionary destruction from the cathedral and restored its "harmony," as some have observed.

As much as Viollet-le-Duc and Lassus may have won the commission to restore Notre-Dame on the grounds that they would be much more scrupulous in their approach than their predecessors had been, and although they emphasized structural repairs over decoration, this account shows that there was nonetheless a great deal of importance attached to giving more sculptural richness to the altered and battered main façade. Further, Viollet-le-Duc and Lassus also undertook a restoration of the nave, transept, and choir that was directed at making the interior more visually appealing while returning some portions to what the two men considered to be their original appearances.

The Interior of Notre-Dame Transformed

Later, this work would be controversial because it was based only loosely on archaeological evidence, and justified in statements by Viollet-le-Duc which historian Chantal Hardy calls "contradictory" (in her article: "Les Roses dans l'Élévation de Notre-Dame de Paris," *Bulletin Monumental* tome 149, n°2 [1991]:153-199). Between 1845 and 1860, the architects inserted twenty-two small new rose windows, on the interior in the tribune level of the nave and transept near the crossing, and on the exterior at the tribune level of the choir.

In 1845-46, the architects restored the windows on the south side of the choir, at the tribune level of the first three bays, as well as in the first bay of the south arm of the transept. Several years later, as work was continuing on the south side of the choir, around the fifth and sixth flying buttresses, the architects discovered above the tribune vaults, in walls built in the thirteenth century, fragments of three rose windows. They believed that the tribunes of the choir had originally been lit by these rose windows but that they had later been removed. This change brought larger windows above the level of the first-story arcade and it reduced the four stories of the interior wall to three. A partial restoration of these rose windows was proposed for the choir; however, because of the work stoppage, only the rose window of the fourth bay on the south side of the choir was completed by 1853.

Another discovery, in July 1854, showed that the original elevation of the nave had also been four stories with small rose windows at the level of the tribunes. This discovery motivated the construction, later in 1854, of three rose windows on the south side of the building —one in the last bay of the nave and two in the west wall of the transept. Windows in corresponding positions on the north side were added in 1857. Two different models of the rose windows were used in 1849 and 1854 respectively; yet a third model was used later for restorations on the exterior of the north side of the choir tribune and on the interior of choir near the transept. The final window restorations were then (c. 1859) carried out on the south side of the choir, where they had begun ten years earlier. Some windows previously restored were replaced to create an alternation between small rose windows representing the first and third alternate designs, as Hardy has explained. Viollet-le-Duc cited archaeological evidence for the restoration of these rose windows, as well as for their particular forms, but more recent archaeology has failed to validate all of his claims.

In the end, what is most telling about this long project to restore the small rose windows is that it demonstrates that the approach Viollet-le-Duc would later describe in his *Dictionary* had informed his work at Notre-Dame much earlier. In bringing the cathedral to the imagined state of completeness he would later describe as the goal of restoration in general, at Notre-Dame, Viollet-le-Duc and Lassus (to some extent) were ready to sacrifice actual, historic fabric for restorations often based either on scant physical or historical evidence. In some instances, there was little documentation available to support the restoration of a certain element, so it was inferred from features elsewhere in the building, or even in other buildings from roughly the same period. Although French government agencies in the 1840s and after touted a new archaeological approach to architectural restoration that stuck to the repair or replacement of elements that had manifestly existed, in contrast to the discredited classicists who had worked on medieval buildings during the eighteenth and early nineteenth centuries, in fact there was still a strong will to make neglected or abused monuments look more presentable. That was certainly the case for Notre-Dame which was promoted as a Gothic building of national significance.

The Restoration of Stained Glass

Key to Viollet-le-Duc's conception of the cathedral's restored interior was the insertion of new stained glass to replace the clear glazing that had been installed throughout the building in the eighteenth century. This alteration Viollet-le-Duc considered to be the worst of all the changes the cathedral had endured over the centuries, as he argued in the monograph on the building he authored with Ferdinand de Guilhermy in 1856. He maintained that the thirteenth-century architect who had lengthened the upper windows in the nave and choir had only done so with the idea that they would be filled with stained glass, not with clear glazing. Thus, the restoration of the stained glass was essential to recreating the original experience of the cathedral. Bercé has described how this aspect of the project unfolded between 1855 and 1875 following the completion of the major architectural undertakings. About a half dozen glass painters were contracted to produce new colored windows for the cathedral and they worked from their own designs. The sacristy built by Viollet-le-Duc and Lassus also eventually had stained glass. However, on the occasion of the imperial baptism on March 16, 1856 the project was just getting off the ground so imitation stained glass was painted on translucent paper and stretched across the window openings, creating in Mérimée's mind (as Camille notes), "a true church of the thirteenth century."

Many of the stained glass artists who worked on the restoration of the windows at Notre-Dame already had experience from similar projects at St.-Denis and the Sainte-Chapelle, as Annie Auzas has described (in *Notre-Dame de Paris*, 2012-19). The three original rose windows —at either end of the transept and at the west façade— were priorities for restoration as they were the principal remnants of the thirteenth-century glass. The rose at the main (west) façade had been heavily restored in the sixteenth century, the one at the north repaired in 1782-83, and the south rose window restored in 1726-27. These were stabilized under Viollet-le-Duc who also led the introduction of new stained glass with historical themes in the choir and chevet to replace the clear glass. Among the personages represented were supporters of the cathedral, the Catholic church in France, and Biblical figures; they included Maurice de Sully, Louis IX, Saint Denis, and Saints Matthew and Mark.

The second half of the 1850s also witnessed the installation of new stained glass windows in the paired lancet windows of the nave and the rose windows that sat above each pair. However, in 1937, on the occasion of the international exposition in Paris that year, twelve prominent stained glass artists were chosen to execute new windows to replace the nineteenth-century restorations. They were unveiled in 1939 and unleashed a storm of controversy which turned on the historic significance of the nineteenth-century replacements for the lost medieval windows. At the core of the debate was a question which restorers still face at Notre-Dame: Is the nineteenth-century restoration itself historically significant and worthy of preservation?

Recalling Viollet-le-Duc's memorable childhood experience at Notre-Dame —when the image of the rose window and the sound of the organ came together— it is perhaps not surprising that the architect restored the great organ as part of his preservation campaign. Philippe Lefebvre (in *Notre-Dame de Paris*, 2012-19) documents the presence of an organ going all the way back to the thirteenth century. The instrument which Viollet-le-Duc found at the outset of his restoration project dated to the 1730s and had been installed above the main entrance, partially obscuring the rose window of the west façade. Already in poor condition during the Revolutionary period, the organ was restored in the early 1830s, but thirty years later it required another substantial restoration. In the early 1860s there was extensive discussion within the government administration and with Viollet-le-Duc about the particular form the new organ should take and about the considerable expense involved in the project. Not until December, 1867 was it completed. By that time, the bulk of the restoration imagined more than twenty years earlier by Viollet-le-Duc and Lassus had been carried out. When the structure was stabilized, the windows filled with colored glass, and the organ restored, it was possible to enjoy a multi-sensory experience of Notre-Dame's interior.

The Spire of Notre-Dame

The exterior was still lacking one element that made it complete in Viollet-le-Duc's estimation. As the window project was ongoing, one of the late —but extremely significant— additions to Notre-Dame, was made in the course of its definitive nineteenth-century restoration: the spire at the crossing. Almost 160 years later, millions worldwide would watch it crash to the roof below on April 15, 2019.

The exterior appearance of Notre-Dame after a substantial amount of restoration had taken place but prior to the reconstruction of the spire, is captured in an 1854 etching by Charles Méryon (1821-1868). The view shows the completed sacristy to the south of the cathedral, although the vantage point is too distant to make it possible to identify many other salient details —apart from the absence of the spire. Méryon's view from the Left Bank does, however, demonstrate the visibility of the cathedral and its prominence in the changing city. The process of Paris's transformation during the Second Empire is one of the leitmotifs of Méryon's masterful prints from the first half of the 1850s, in which he often captured elements of the city that were being eradicated by modernization. The 1854 etching of Notre-Dame focuses on the apse (the east end), whereas an earlier view, from 1850 (the *Petit-Pont*, or *Little-Bridge*) showed the building from the opposite perspective, from the west, with the cathedral's towers looming over the dense fabric of the Île de la Cité. Méryon thus registered in his prints the changing presentation of Notre-Dame in which its isolation and completeness as an image of Gothic architecture were both being enhanced. As one had centuries before, a new Notre-Dame was emerging gradually from the fabric of an earlier building, and Viollet-le-Duc's next major project for the cathedral would hasten that emergence.

Why was reconstructing a crossing spire a priority for Viollet-le-Duc, given that it was neither necessary to the structural integrity of the building nor to its religious function? The answer is that the spire was absolutely crucial to Notre-Dame's appearance, in the estimation of many, and it was central to its urban presence. In the illustrations to his *Entretiens sur l'Architecture* (*Lectures on Architecture*) published in 1864, Viollet-le-Duc showed an ideal Notre-Dame with twin spires at the west (front) façade as well as one at the crossing. In the *Entretiens*, Viollet-le-Duc noted that as beautiful as Notre-Dame then appeared (in the 1860s), it would have been even more so if its Gothic builders had placed spires on top of the towers at the façade. In the nineteenth century, rebuilding three spires would have given form to the cathedral in an imagined state of completeness, and therefore might have fit well with Viollet-le-Duc's conception of restoration, but the architect did not go so far as to propose creating the entire group; instead, his focus remained on the crossing tower. To propose the restoration of even this one spire was audacious, given the perennial lack of funds for Notre-Dame. But the architect's insistence on this aspect of the project demonstrates just how essential spires were felt to be to Gothic buildings at the time.

Gothic Spires in the Nineteenth Century

Indeed, of the nineteenth-century restoration projects that dealt with medieval churches and cathedrals, many comprised the restoration of spires which had frequently fallen victim to damage from the elements, from extreme weather events (like lightning strikes), and from Revolutionary vandalism. As Jean-Michel Leniaud concludes, "The nineteenth century was the century of the spire" (in "Les Flèches au XIXe Siècle," *L'Archange, la Flèche* [Caisse Nationale des Monuments Historiques et des Sites, 1987]). Government-sponsored restorations of churches and cathedrals in mid-nineteenth century France tried to avoid work that was purely "decorative," and to focus instead on structural repairs, but architects and administrators could not give up on spires: they were key elements that carried both religious and urban meanings.

Prior to reconstructing the spire of Notre-Dame, Viollet-le-Duc had worked at the nearby Sainte-Chapelle where the reconstruction of the spire was also an important element of the restoration. It enhanced the exquisite jewel box of a building and made its presence known within the densely-built environment of the Île de la Cité. The architect was also familiar with what would have been a negative example, of how *not* to rebuild a spire, embodied by the replacement planned for Rouen Cathedral following a fire that destroyed its spire in 1822. Support for rebuilding that spire ran incredibly strong among the people of the industrialized port city in Normandy. A project for a structurally daring replacement (some 148 m. in height) made out of cast iron got under way soon after the fire but foundered following the death of its architect, Jean-Antoine Alavoine (1778-1834), amid growing criticism from government funding and oversight agencies. Viollet-le-Duc was one of the loudest critics of the cast-iron spire, which he faulted on structural and aesthetic grounds, and he played a role in curtailing funding for it in 1848. Only the personal intervention of President of the Republic Marshall MacMahon in 1875 brought about its completion. In the interim, the period in which the spire stood partly finished, the Rouennais considered it to be a stain on their city. While a completed spire that soared above the skyline proclaimed the prosperity and high moral standing of a place, critics believed, an unfinished one suggested just the opposite. And if a spire marked the presence of a church or cathedral in a dense urban area, the lack of one meant that the monument threatened to disappear, or at the very least, it could fail to provide a point of orientation for inhabitants and visitors.

A project for a reconstructed spire at Notre-Dame was made by Lassus before his death, based on seventeenth-century views of the cathedral. It would have had a one-story openwork base surmounted by gables and an octagonal spire, but was not carried out because Lassus was uncertain about the documentation on which his project rested. After the death of his collaborator in 1857, Viollet-le-Duc proposed a restoration of the spire in the style of the thirteenth century, with two openwork stories resting on a solid base.

Believed to date from around 1250, the original spire had been thirty meters tall and surmounted by an iron cross. It was blown down by a windstorm in 1606 but was put back in place the same year. In the mid-1740s it was found to be in a poor condition that only worsened until it was finally taken down in 1797. Still, as Élisabeth Pillet has detailed (in *Notre-Dame de Paris*, 2012-19) fragments of the original spire survived to guide Viollet-le-Duc's restoration and confirm the thirteenth-century date. The design was approved on March 8, 1858 and the construction carried out by the contractor Auguste Bellu, who had rebuilt the spire of Sainte-Chapelle under Lassus's direction, assisted by the carpenter Henri Georges. The new spire was inaugurated in 1859.

The oak (from the Champagne region) structure of the spire rested on the four piers around the crossing below. The openings at the second story were surmounted by gables and pinnacles above which rose the spire itself. Decorated with projecting leaves, the spire culminated in an iron cross and Gallic Coq (found, in damaged condition, after the 2019 fire). The spire and supporting structure were sheathed in lead and the decorative elements were made of lead, including the sixteen gargoyles that served as spouts for rainwater at the level of each platform below the spire. The spire rose, according to Viollet-le-Duc, forty-four and a half meters from the ridge pole of the roof to the Gallic Coq.

In the four valleys where the roofs of the nave, choir, and transept intersected at the crossing, figures of the twelve Apostles and four Evangelists stepped up to the base of the spire. The figures were made by Geoffroy-Dechaume. As Deirdre Westgate and Charanne Clarke have pointed out, the architect and sculptor had collaborated to recreate the medieval stone sculpture on the cathedral's exterior but had not previously made free-standing copper sculptures. The production of these sculptures (each weighing about 500 pounds) was motivated by Viollet-le-Duc's discovery of "sixteen vertical crown posts" that projected outward from the original wooden structure that supported the spire. These then became the bases for the sculptures. The figures themselves were made by creating plaster molds into which iron was cast; the iron forms were then used to hammer out the copper leaves into human form. The resulting hollow sculptures were supported by interior iron armatures. The representation of the Apostle St. Thomas was based on Viollet-le-Duc's own face and he was shown holding an architect's rule with Latin inscriptions identifying Viollet as the builder of the spire. The copper figures were completed in1861 and stood on their original perches until the week prior to the April 15, 2019 fire. At that point, they were, fortuitously, taken down and transported to the Dordogne region for storage and eventual restoration.

Shortly after the completion of the spire, in April 1860, Viollet-le-Duc felt compelled to write an article in the *Gazette des Beaux-arts* defending himself from the accusations he said he had been subjected to by forgetful Parisians who couldn't recall the previous spire which had been taken down more than sixty years earlier. Far from it being the product of his own imagination, wrote Viollet-le-Duc, the new spire was a restoration of the original one that had stood until relatively recently when its deteriorated condition had caused Godde to demolish it. He described the structure of the restored spire and its decorative elements in great detail, and proudly announced that in a recent and violent wind storm the spire had only swayed twenty centimeters. Clearly, the spire was for looking *at* —not *from*— but nonetheless there was interior access to the two lower stories. However, cautioned the architect, unless there were a substantial change to ladies' fashions, women would be unlikely to be able to get their stylishly wide skirts through the trap door to the spire's second story as it was no more than seventy centimeters in diameter.

The Île de la Cité Reimagined

If a lady or gentleman had been able to climb up to the second story of the spire, she or he could have looked out around the cathedral and seen a site that was in the process of transformation. Not only was the entire city of Paris in the throes of Haussmannization, but Notre-Dame's immediate surroundings were also being fundamentally altered. That alteration —specifically, the creation of open space around the cathedral— reflected an entirely novel understanding of the building's optimal relationship to its setting. Before the nineteenth century, the spire and towers of Notre-Dame rose above a sea of buildings and roofs; with the new concept of restoration in the mid-nineteenth century, there emerged a belief among government architects and administrators that restored buildings should be easily and completely visible, free from encumbrances.

In the plan of Paris that was produced by its reorganization under Napoleon III and Haussmann, Notre-Dame occupied an important spot on the Île de la Cité. The cathedral could be seen from both the Left and Right banks of the Seine and it marked the intersection of east–west and north–south axes that had their origins in the Roman street plan. Making Notre-Dame visible was thus important to the rebuilding of Paris in the Second Empire, and it also fit into the general emphasis on the visibility of restored buildings expressed by the government architecture agencies from the July Monarchy onward. The term used to describe the process of clearing a space around an historic monument was "isolation."

As early as April 12, 1832 the Parisian newspaper *Le Globe* called for the virtual eradication of the neighborhoods along the Seine, which were considered to be disease-ridden cesspools. Those quarters, the writer argued, could only be "cleaned up by the almost total destruction of the houses on the Île de la Cité, the quays and all the little adjacent streets." The sanitary argument, which saw the Île de la Cité as the "infected" heart of the city, was accompanied by another view of the place of the monument in Paris, expressed shortly thereafter in *Le Globe*. The banks of the Seine, according to the paper, were where new arrivals from elsewhere in France and Europe headed when they came to Paris. "The Isle of Notre Dame," *Le Globe* proposed, should be transformed into a "riante promenade," something like a "smiling pleasure ground," "where the central populations of the metropolis [...] can easily come to breathe the fresh air, at each return of the July sun. A quiet wood would cover the destruction wrecked on the Palace of the Archbishop [sacked during the July Revolution, and] on the walls of Notre-Dame." The city of Paris thus purchased the site of the former archbishop's palace adjacent to the cathedral in 1837 to create a planted and fenced "promenade." The site of violent political conflict thus became a place where residents and visitors alike could stroll, taking in one of Paris's most renowned monuments.

Once it was cleared, the south side of the cathedral could accommodate the guardian's house, or the presbytery, which Viollet-le-Duc designed in 1866 and completed the following year. Georges and Olivier Poisson point out in their biography of Viollet-le-Duc that this building, constructed twenty years after the nearby sacristy and without the collaboration of

Lassus, is very different in conception than the earlier structure. While the exterior of the sacristy mimicked the Rayonnant architecture of the cathedral, the guardian's house was clearly nineteenth-century. In no way did it reproduce a medieval building and had more in common with contemporary urban and suburban houses in the neo-Gothic mode. Still, details like the tapering chimney on the gable end and the oriel windows make the building distinctive. In addition to providing lodgings for the cathedral's guardian, the building also contained office space.

As the restoration of the cathedral was entering its final phase, with the reconstruction of the spire and the recreation of the stained glass, the *parvis* was cleared and extended, which complemented the gardens that had been created along the south side of the cathedral, around the new sacristy, and at the east end. In fact, the city of Paris had objected a decade earlier, in 1845, to the placement of the new sacristy to the south of the nave on the grounds that it would interfere with the public use of the area between the cathedral and the river. Thus, at the point that Viollet-le-Duc's and Lassus's project was beginning, the site was already being thought of in a new way, as a space of recreation with its amenities being the historic building and the river. Jean-Michel Leniaud has suggested (in *Autour de Notre-Dame* [2003]) that Viollet-le-Duc and Lassus were encouraged to conceive of Notre-Dame in its setting in the way that English cathedrals had often been, "rising in the midst of a vast green lawn surrounded by buildings of the same style."

In its new park-like setting, the restored Notre-Dame de Paris stood isolated and fully available for viewing by tourists and residents alike. But some critics failed to appreciate the transformation of the site and thought that Notre-Dame had also lost some of its religious significance through its isolation. Jean-Philippe Schmit, for example, who wrote from a Catholic perspective, considered the isolation of Notre-Dame to be a loss to the symbolic importance it had formerly held when it loomed over, or gathered around it, a sea of smaller buildings. With the surrounding structures cleared away, Schmit already anticipated in 1837 (in his book *Les Eglises Gothiques*) before the major restoration had begun that Notre-Dame, which already looked like a "great elephant in the middle of the desert," would soon be "no more than a crouching dromedary." Moreover, set apart from its surroundings and incorporated into the network of new streets and avenues that Haussmann had created, Notre-Dame de Paris was fully engaged, by the time its restoration was finished, into the fabric of Second Empire Paris. That new Paris, as critics and historians have suggested, was designed for consumption by the city's ascendant bourgeois class and relatively affluent tourists, and was less and less available to the neighborhood's former working-class inhabitants. Notre-Dame de Paris would become a central attraction in a spectacular city in which, as

Schmit put it, one would stop into the cathedral just as one stopped into the museum. Both would then be cultural attractions and the cathedral consequently drained of its religious relevance.

It may be that Schmit's concern was over-stated; after all, Notre-Dame continues to be an important site for Catholics the world over. But he was not wrong in predicting that as a consequence of its mid-nineteenth century restoration, the cathedral of Paris would be seen as one of the capital's most important cultural attractions, a must-see for residents and tourists alike. Among the latter was the American artist Winslow Homer who visited Notre-Dame just as the restoration was being completed and who made a humorous sketch on one of the towers in 1867; he followed up with a larger painting titled *Gargoyles at Notre-Dame* (1867) in a private collection. The sketch, in the collection of the Cooper-Hewitt Museum in New York shows a stern-looking man in a tricorn hat trying to lure a kitten off the end of a gargoyle. The building Homer and his contemporaries came to view and experience was an image of the Gothic as seen through the eyes of the nineteenth century, and in particular, the Gothic as conceived of by the restoration's architects Viollet-le-Duc and Lassus. A key feature of that nineteenth-century building —its spire— disappeared in April, 2019, leaving us with a question which restorers have faced at Notre-Dame for close to two centuries: What is the historic monument which should be preserved for posterity?

Chapter 7

The Modern Notre-Dame

The "Structural Rationalism" of the Gothic

Eugène-Emmanuel Viollet-le-Duc arguably did more than any other nineteenth-century designer or theorist to promote the relevance of Gothic architecture as a model for contemporary building. In specific, he argued that medieval masons and the buildings they constructed could tell the nineteenth century how to engage with new building materials then being developed, or with old ones being perfected. Among those materials were iron (and eventually, steel), concrete, and plate glass. Viollet-le-Duc and other theorists worried that modern builders too often used the new resources in ways that were essentially conservative, to the extent that they mimicked traditional construction in stone and wood. For instance, from the time that cast iron was used extensively as a building material, in the mid-nineteenth century, it was frequently molded into historical forms like classical columns or Gothic arches. In opposition to what he saw as these retardataire uses of the new materials, Viollet-le-Duc instead insisted they should be employed following the conceptual approach of medieval masons —not the specific forms they used.

In the first volume of his *Entretiens sur l'Architecture* (*Lectures on Architecture*, 1863), Viollet-le-Duc argued that classical architecture was not useful in providing a model for how to use "certain materials [that] modern industry has furnished, such as iron." By way of contrast, he maintained that lay architects of the late twelfth century —that is, the pioneers of the Gothic style— had provided "principles and methods" that could be seamlessly adapted to "these new materials as well as to all the requirements that reveal themselves daily at the core of our society." Viollet-le-Duc credited medieval architects with a "sincerity" lacking in their modern counterparts because the buildings they constructed always fit their functions: they never made palaces look like churches, or made hospitals look like palaces, and so on. Moreover, the applicability of thirteenth-century architecture to modern architectural challenges derived from the fact that early Gothic builders had developed their "principles" from rational considerations rather than from a given set of forms. Viollet-le-Duc also said, more pointedly, that "It must be stated at the outset that it is impossible to separate the form of thirteenth-century architecture from its structure; every member of this architecture is the consequence of a structural requirement, just as in the plant or animal world there is not a phenomenon, not an appendage that is not the product of an organic necessity [...]." This concept of Gothic architecture, often referred to as "structural rationalism," has frequently been credited to Viollet-le-Duc who considered even such evidently decorative Gothic elements as gargoyles to have played structural, or at least practical, roles in the overall designs of the buildings. (Gargoyles, he maintained, fulfilled the important function of helping shed rainwater from the roofs of churches and cathedrals.) This structurally rational approach to design, ostensibly pioneered in the Gothic period, could then inform the ways that nineteenth-century architects responded to the novel requirements of the modern world while also capitalizing on the materials that industry had provided.

Modernism in Architecture

Responding to modernity, embracing new materials, and eschewing mere imitations of historic forms: these were all aspects of modernism in architecture and the visual arts more generally.

Modernism as an architectural phenomenon was connected to, but distinct from, its manifestations in music, literature, and the other visual arts from the late nineteenth century into the twentieth. Modernism was often believed to be "revolutionary," both aesthetically and politically, and to involve the rejection of tradition. Viollet-le-Duc played an important role in the development of modernism in architecture by making the surprising argument that the way toward a truly modern architecture had been pointed out by medieval builders. He certainly did not discount historic architecture as a source of inspiration, but he did reject historicism as it was practiced by those of his contemporaries who imitated older buildings in new materials. Instead, he sought to extract from historic architecture —specifically, the Gothic— principles that could be applied to contemporary building.

Viollet-le-Duc's theory of modern architecture was influential and there were any number of artists and architects who approached Notre-Dame with his perspective in mind. His claims of a conceptual connection between the Gothic builder and the modern engineer (or progressive architect) was echoed over and over. For instance, the sculptor Raymond Duchamp-Villon (1876-1918) asked in a 1914 essay entitled "L'Architecture et le Fer" ("Architecture and Iron") "Is there not a surprising similarity between the conceptions of engineers working in steel and those of medieval masons?" He continued, "Do we not find in both the same boundless ambition always to achieve the greater, the taller, the more daring? Across from Gothic Notre-Dame, the true tower of modern Paris rises on the Champs de Mars [the Eiffel Tower]. Both works, the tower and the nave, are born of the same desire to build and both fulfill a similar dream of superhuman exaltation." By the time the Eiffel Tower was constructed, for the international exposition that celebrated the centennial of the French Revolution in 1889, Viollet-le-Duc had already argued that modern engineers (like Gustave Eiffel) were the conceptual heirs to medieval builders; by the World War I era that idea was widely accepted.

Church and State at Notre-Dame

The reconceptualization of Notre-Dame as embodying a vision for the future, rather than just an image of the past, represented a profound rethinking of the monument's significance. By the time that transition in the estimation of Notre-Dame took place, the legal status of the building had also changed in important ways. First, the law that established the separation of church in state in France passed by the Chamber of Deputies on December 9, 1905, made Notre-Dame state property. Second, by the terms of a law passed on December 31, 1913 the cathedral was officially designated a "monument historique." Legal scholar Mathilde Roellinger explains that "after the statute of 9th December 1905, called the Loi de separation des Églises et de l'État, which put an end to the subsidies from [the] State to churches, these latter were left without resources or protection" ("Centenary of the French Law on Historic Monuments," *Art Antiquity & Law*, vol. 19, no. 4, 2014, p. 327+). Roellinger credits Victor Hugo with having laid the groundwork for the state's 1913 legislation, which articulated a public interest in privately-owned historic buildings, when he stated in 1832 that "There are two things in an edifice, its use and its beauty. Its use belongs to the owner but its beauty belongs to everyone." The public interest in Notre-Dame was recognized by its official designation in 1913 as an historic monument; that was an official acknowledgment that its "beauty" (among other qualities) was important to the public, regardless of their religious affiliations. This status reflects the success of Viollet-le-Duc and his collaborators in making Notre-Dame into a secular image of the French nation and its cultural achievements.

Viewing Notre-Dame as a primarily secular monument was a way of getting around the tense politics of church and state during the Third Republic (1870-1940) which followed the collapse of the Second Empire of Napoléon III. Maylis Curie has written (in Glaser, ed., *The Idea of the Gothic*

Cathedral, 2018) that it was "a period of intense antagonisms between church and state. In a context of widespread anticlericalism on [the] one hand and strong Catholicism on the other, with many different positions in between, Gothic cathedrals were held up as symbols of the various ideals circulating at the time, manifesting the opinions and ideologies of those who promoted them politically or artistically." Thus, the Decadent author who converted to Catholicism, J.-K. Huysmans, could write an avowedly religious, even mystical, appreciation of Gothic architecture in *La Cathédrale* (*The Cathedral*, 1898) and the influential scholar Émile Mâle (1862-1954) could publish his contemporaneous, pioneering art historical study, *L'Art Religieux du XIIIe Siècle en France* (*Religious Art of the Thirteenth Century in France*, 1898), both just prior to the turn of the twentieth century.

An Impressionist's Notre-Dame

The appearance of these books followed by a decade the American Impressionist painter Childe Hassam's (1859-1935) canvas *Notre Dame Cathedral, Paris, 1888*. His painting confirms Curie's suggestion that Gothic architecture could be viewed from a wide range of perspectives during the Third Republic since the painting is neither a religious celebration nor an architectural documentation. Instead, Hassam recognizes the important urban role that had been accorded to Notre-Dame through the process of its nineteenth-century restoration.

Like many American painters at the end of the nineteenth and the beginning of the twentieth centuries, Hassam was drawn to Paris as the preeminent artistic center of the West at that time. Further, his painting style was deeply influenced by that of the French Impressionists who had risen to visibility in a series of group exhibitions in Paris that began in 1874 and continued until 1886, just before Hassam painted his view of Notre-Dame. Although the slate of exhibitors changed from one exhibition to another, and included artists whom we would not today label "Impressionists," there were a number of key figures whose work has come to represent the style: Claude Monet, Edgar Degas, Pierre-Auguste Renoir, Camille Pissarro, Berthe Morisot, Mary Cassatt, and Gustave Caillebotte. They pioneered the technique that Hassam adopts in his representation of Notre-Dame. As he does, they made art that captured a momentary, fleeting view of a particular subject, and they did so by deploying their paint on the canvas with relatively hurried and visible brushstrokes. The colors the Impressionists used represented what they understood to be the variety of tones that blended in the eye when one saw an object in "real" life. Hence, Hassam emphasizes the steam or smoke that rises from the boats tied up at the quay of the Seine, invisible below street level, as well as the clouds that blow from north to south behind and above the cathedral.

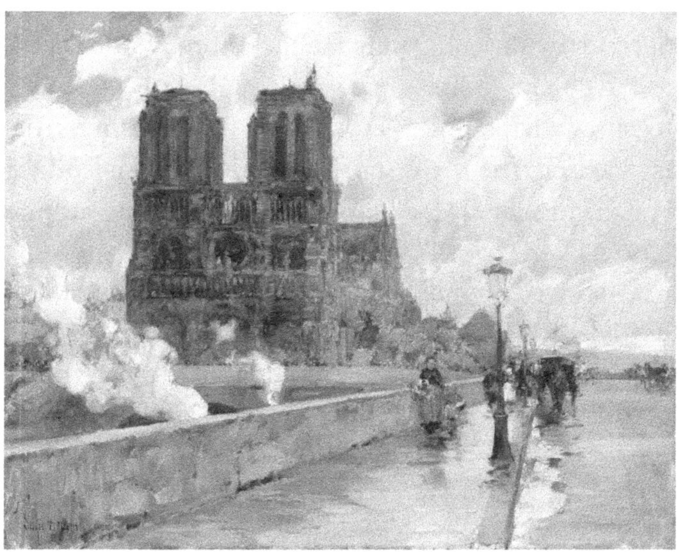

12. Childe Frederick Hassam, *Notre Dame Cathedral, Paris*, 1888 (oil on canvas).

Hassam's view is both typical and atypical of Notre-Dame pictures from the nineteenth and twentieth centuries. First, he takes a common viewing position well to the west of the cathedral on the Left Bank. That allows him to lead the viewer's eye into the picture with the diagonal line of the wall along the quay. The gas lamps along the sidewalk —one of the innovations of Haussmann's Paris— punctuate that diagonal and as they get smaller, receding into the middle- and background, they emphasize the deep space of the picture. The street in Hassam's picture also plays its usual roles in the city: it is a space of circulation (as made clear by the horse-drawn carriages) and of commerce (as demonstrated by the flower-seller with her long apron and child in tow).

Second, by stepping quite far back from Notre-Dame, as have many other image-makers, Hassam was able to show virtually the entirety of the building. That is precisely the view that Viollet-le-Duc and others sought to make possible by clearing the site around Notre-Dame.

Many elements of the site that were the result of its recent restoration are clearly shown by Hassam, including the sacristy, the garden at the south side of the building, and the plantings at the front of the building on the expanded *parvis*. Like many images of Notre-Dame from the second half of the nineteenth century, Hassam shows the building to be both timeless and contemporary. The façade is dark and solid, despite the overall brushy handling of paint, yet the amenities around Notre-Dame would have been recognized as relatively recent additions to the site —the plantings, sacristy, and so on. Finally, as in many Impressionist pictures of Paris's new and old architecture, in Hassam's the steam clouds —as ephemeral as they are— have the capacity to block out the stolid cathedral; a puff even obscures the restored tympanum of the main portal. One is tempted to invoke here Karl Marx and Friedrich Engel's famous description of modernity (in the *Communist Manifesto*, 1848) as the age in which "all that is solid melts into air."

Shortly after Hassam completed his view of Notre-Dame, Monet (1840-1926) embarked, in 1892, on the most famous series of Gothic cathedral paintings produced in the nineteenth century. Several years later, in 1895, he exhibited twenty of what was by then a group of thirty paintings of the façade of Rouen Cathedral. As the major scholar of Monet's series pictures, Paul Hayes Tucker, has observed (in the exhibition catalogue from the Museum of Fine Arts, Boston, *Monet in the '90s, the Series Paintings*, 1989) Rouen Cathedral was not considered a masterwork of the Gothic, but its long construction history did reflect the entire development of the style, from its beginnings in the twelfth century to its culmination in the Perpendicular Gothic of the fifteenth and sixteenth centuries. Like Notre-Dame de Paris, Rouen Cathedral had also been the subject of a protracted —and controversial— restoration campaign which included the reconstruction of its spire out of cast iron. That very prominent, and in some critics' estimations, very ugly, part of the building would have only been recently completed when Monet arrived on the scene. He mostly ignored the spire and only included it in the scant images that show the entire cathedral from a distance. In contrast to Hassam who stood back from Notre-Dame to capture the entire monument, Monet nearly always got very close to it, homing in on the highly-decorated façade to depict the changing colors of the carved stonework over the course of the day.

Like the other major Impressionists, Monet (as Sylvain Amic has observed in *Cathédrales, 1789-1914, Un Mythe Moderne*, 2014) ignored Notre-Dame de Paris, perhaps associating it with Victor Hugo and the

Romantic movement of the early nineteenth century, which was by then passé. Amic notes that Camille Pissarro, the Impressionist painter of "boulevards, squares, the Louvre and the Tuileries, turned his back on it." What to make of this shunning of Notre-Dame on the part of artists who were generally preoccupied with painting the new attractions of Haussmannized Paris? Their "precursor" Johan Barthold Jongkind (1819-1891) painted several atmospheric views of Notre-Dame in the early-to-mid 1850s and in 1864 even depicted, in a very long view of the cathedral from a distant point on the quay on the Left Bank, its recently-completed spire, in a painting in the collection of the Musée d'Orsay. Notre-Dame was also the subject of numerous canvases by Jean-François Raffaëlli (1850-1924) who was a controversial inclusion in the Impressionist exhibitions of 1880 and 1881. He was promoted by Degas but disapproved of, along with several other realists included in the shows, by Monet and others. Possibly, Notre-Dame was rejected as a subject by the Impressionists because many other artists, like Raffaëlli, who were also inspired by French Impressionism, chose to paint the cathedral. Examples include the Venetian painter Sylvius Paoletti (1864-1921) and the American Henry Ossawa Tanner (1859-1937). The Rouen native Albert Lebourg (1849-1928), who participated in several Impressionist exhibitions but who was not part of the core group, depicted Notre-Dame several times, but not until the mid-1890s, after the completion of Monet's successful Rouen Cathedral series. Lebourg always showed the building from the same classic vantage point to the east of the cathedral and on the Left Bank from where it was possible to depict the entire monument and to focus on its flying buttresses. By restoring the striking Gothic structure —especially its buttresses— and topping it with a new spire, Viollet-le-Duc had set up a view of the building that became ubiquitous, even a cliché, which may explain why some artists avoided it.

Notre-Dame and Modern Art

It was not until the first decade of the twentieth century that Notre-Dame was rediscovered and reinvented as a subject for avant-garde art. At that point, in the years following the law separating church and state, painters fully embraced the abstraction of the cathedral's forms that had been hinted at in Hassam's 1888 picture where the sculpted elements of the façade were blurred by his broad brushstrokes. Among the more prolific painters of Notre-Dame just after the turn of the century was Francis Picabia (1879-1953) who had trained at the École des Beaux-arts and elsewhere in the 1890s, and who first exhibited his work at the Salon des Artistes Français in 1894. Although he was eventually associated with the Cubist and Dada movements, in the first decade of the twentieth century, Picabia experimented with a number of different styles, including a late version of Impressionism. In 1905-06 he painted several views of the façade of Notre-Dame and took a somewhat elevated position on the Left Bank from where he recorded the late-day sun on the west elevation. He also positioned himself so that he could see, and emphasize, the spire. In one atypical canvas, named *Notre-Dame le Matin no.1* from 1906, Picabia showed the façade in shadow, at a time of day when the sun was at the east. The emphasis on different effects of light and color seen in the paintings, even the title of the painting that keyed it to a particular time of day, suggest Picabia's awareness of the earlier paintings of Rouen Cathedral by Monet. In a slightly later painting, from 1908, he adopted a very low perspective on Notre-Dame which placed him at the level of the Seine's waters, from the east of the building. By doing so he was able to exaggerate the height of the spire which he also showed in great detail.

E. Phillips Fox (1865-1915) adopted a similar perspective on Notre-Dame in a painting produced around 1906-07 now in the collection of the National Gallery of Victoria in Melbourne.The Australian artist had moved between his home country, London, and Paris for two decades before settling in the French capital with his wife, Ethel Carrick Fox (1872-1952), who was also an artist, in 1905. The work is a rarity in Fox's oeuvre, a nocturne that depicts an historic building. Like Picabia, Fox places the viewer on the water, to the east of the cathedral, but because of the darkness —punctuated only by the lights of bridge traffic between the Left Bank and the Île de la Cité—nothing definitive can be made out of the hulking mass of the cathedral, beyond its towers and spire. Other images also made in this important first decade of the twentieth century would similarly abstract Notre-Dame while adopting familiar vantage points on the cathedral.

It is uncertain whether the altered relationship between church and state after 1905 would have made any difference to the artists who came to paint Notre-Dame. However, for at least a handful of fin-de-siècle and early twentieth-century artists, argues Maylis Curie, the contemporary Anarchist movement created a new perception of Gothic cathedrals that did have an impact on how they depicted Notre-Dame and other similar buildings. Curie singles out Pissarro and Maximilien Luce (1858-1941) as two artists who were drawn to Anarchism and also made the representation of Gothic buildings important parts of their production. While Pissarro is well-known for his series of Rouen Cathedral canvases, Luce produced a number of ambitious paintings of Notre-Dame. Anarchism eschewed the republican, nationalistic interpretation of Gothic cathedrals as well as the Catholic view of them. Instead, explains Curie, Anarchists —who "opposed all authoritarian structures, whether societal, political, or religious"—"looked to Gothic cathedrals as products of an anti-hierarchical society, which prized individual freedom and collective labor toward a common good."

Starting in 1898 Luce produced seven paintings of Notre-Dame in his post-Impressionist, Divisionist style, which is characterized by the application of color in dots and patches. Luce shared some of Monet's interests in Gothic architecture to the extent that he observed the play of light on the decorative elements of the façade at different times of day and drew attention to the many colors that danced across the stone. Yet, he stood much farther back from Notre-Dame than Monet had from Rouen Cathedral and even farther back from the cathedral of Paris than had Hassam. By stepping away from Notre-Dame Luce is able to show more of the surrounding activity—people on the *parvis* and surrounding streets. For Curie, that composition enhances Luce's objective of portraying "cathedrals in connection with a harmonious, busy, and peaceful society where individuals can retain their dignity in their occupations and profit from their leisure."

The Fauvists's Notre-Dame

The year 1905, marked by the official separation of church and state in France, was artistically important because that fall the Salon d'Automne included a group of paintings by artists whom critic Louis Vauxcelles (in the journal *Gil Blas*, 17 Oct 1905) dubbed the "fauves," or literally, "beasts." Vauxcelles was responding to the canvases of Henri Matisse, André Derain, Maurice de Vlaminck and others who, from around the turn of the century, had been building on some aspects of Neo-Impressionism toward a kind of painting in which broad, flat areas of vivid colors produced somewhat abstract representations of their subjects. For Vauxcelles, the Fauves' application of paint was jarring, almost violent, and in a word, "beastly."

Notre-Dame with its blocky towers and hulking mass presented an appealing subject for several of the Fauves who painted it repeatedly just as the loosely-affiliated group was achieving critical visibility. Before Vauxcelles stuck his moniker on the group, its recognized leader, Henri Matisse (1869-1954) was already painting Notre-Dame. As Dagmar Kronenberger-Hüffer points out (in *Cathédrales, 1789-1914, Un Mythe Moderne*) Matisse produced what is thought to be his earliest painting of Notre-Dame in 1900 (now in the Tate Gallery, London) from a position quite close to Luce's favored Left Bank vantage point. Doing so allowed for a complete image of the cathedral from the west that included the *parvis* and the Petit Pont in the foreground. Looking down from a higher spot than had Luce, Matisse could show the loiterers on the south bank of the Seine as well as the barge traffic on the river. Like Hassam had, Matisse depicts the smoke or steam from the barges wafting up in front of the cathedral and blocking out his view of a portion of the façade. Two years later, in 1902, Matisse painted Notre-Dame in a way that moved further away from Post-Impressionism and towards Fauvism (in a canvas now in the collection of the Albright-Knox Art Gallery, Buffalo).

Matisse's former studio at number nineteen, Quai Saint-Michel was occupied from 1908 by his friend Albert Marquet (1875-1947), who was from the city of Bourdeaux but came to Paris in 1890 to study art. The two met at the École des Beaux-arts where they were both students of Symbolist painter Gustave Moreau. Prior to World War I, Marquet painted no fewer than twenty-five pictures of Notre-Dame, many from the exact vantage point as had Matisse. Although Marquet used more somber colors than did Matisse, over time he applied them increasingly in broad, flat areas, in the Fauvist manner. Like Luce and the Impressionists before him, Marquet emphasized different weather conditions, and gave some of his Notre-Dame paintings titles that indicated the presence of snow or rain. Kronenberger-Hüffer argues that Marquet may have gravitated to Notre-Dame as a subject because it was a commercially successful one. If that was indeed the case, he owed some of this profitability to Viollet-le-Duc and his contemporaries who had made Notre-Dame and the surrounding site presentable after earlier destruction and decay and who had popularized it as an image of the French nation.

The Modern Notre-Dame and World War I

Among the artists who saw Marquet's work and were informed by it was the young American painter Edward

Hopper (1882-1967) who arrived in Paris in the fall of 1906. Marquet showed work in the Salon d'Automne that year and in early 1907 in a solo exhibition at the Galerie Druet. Hopper's biographer, Gail Levin, maintains that Hopper's dark palette and "prosaic, simplified approach to his subjects" can be traced to his interest in Marquet. Hopper's 1907 painting of Notre-Dame (Whitney Museum of American Art) certainly features the dark green, gold, brown, and gray tones that Marquet also used to depict the cathedral, but Hopper takes the opposite perspective on the building, situating himself to the east of the building.

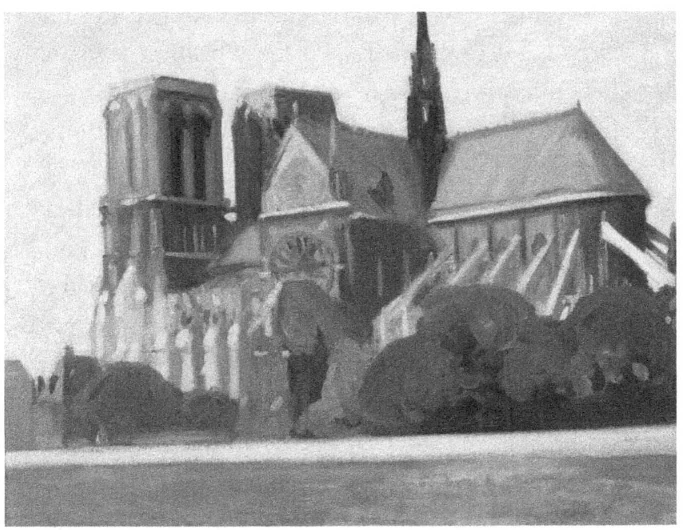

13. Edward Hopper, *Notre-Dame de Paris, Oil on canvas, 1907.*

However much Hopper abstracts the forms of Notre-Dame, he does carefully show us the sacristy and guardian's house to the south of the cathedral, and the plantings around the building nearly engulf the flying buttresses at the nave and apse. By blocking out traffic and pedestrians —key elements of Marquet's views of Notre-Dame— Hopper expresses the British notion of a cathedral rising from a greenspace, the image that its nineteenth-century restorers had had in mind.

The Cathedral of Reims in World War I

The efflorescence of Fauvist and Fauvist-inspired painting of Notre-Dame immediately preceded the outbreak of World War I in July, 1914. The cataclysmic Great War wreaked violence across Europe, led to an estimated forty million civilian and military deaths, and upturned Western civilization. In France and worldwide, the nation's Gothic cathedrals became a potent symbol of German-led destruction. When Reims Cathedral was hit by five German artillery shells on September 18, 1914 and then by more extensive shelling the following day, it started a fire in the north tower. Eventually some 300 shells hit Notre-Dame of Reims and around eighty-five percent of buildings in the surrounding town were destroyed by the end of the war. "A phantom church in the midst of a phantom town" was how Émile Mâle described the scene in Reims in 1917 (quoted by Joëlle Prungnaud in Glaser, ed., *The Idea of the Gothic Cathedral*, 2018). Echoing the rhetoric that surrounded the destruction of historic buildings at the time of the French Revolution, Mâle decried the "vandalisme allemande" ("German vandalism") that nearly reduced Reims to rubble.

By the outbreak of war in 1914, Matisse had returned to his studio on the Quai Saint-Michel and that year he produced two paintings of Notre-Dame, one of which is now in the collection of the Museum of Modern Art in New York. At the time of its acquisition by MoMA, curator William Rubin wrote eloquently (in a statement preserved in a press release from April 22, 1975) that the painting is "vigorously brushed, its surface enlivened by a bold scumbling and its drawing dominated by powerful black architectonic lines whose scaffolding testifies to Matisse's ability to absorb Cubism without imitating it." The building itself is placed at the upper left-hand corner of the canvas and it is "radically simplified" into two massive rectangles, fulfilling a movement towards an increasingly abstracted view of Notre-Dame initiated in Matisse's paintings from ten years earlier. As Rubin points out, the north tower and the base of the south tower are shaded with a scratching (or scumbling) produced by the hard end of a brush. The south quay of the Seine is suggested by a simple, black diagonal line which runs to a single smudge of green to indicate the plantings at the south of the cathedral, while the Petit Pont is reduced to one curving line that supports two horizontal black strokes. These black lines "cool" the blue, as Matisse put it. Rubin summarizes: "In the brilliance and daring of its drawing, the economy of its abstraction, and the assertive liberty of its scumbled technique *Notre-Dame* is an exceptional, almost unique work in Matisse's *oeuvre*, and in its handling and conception adumbrates much that would happen in painting half a century later." By paring down the scene to its essential volumes and lines, and by emphasizing the means by which he had manipulated the pigment on the surface of the canvas (for instance, by scratching away at the paint), Matisse anticipated (says Rubin) later modernist painting, undoubtedly thinking of mid-century Abstract Expressionism.

Matisse's second campaign of painting Notre-Dame coincided with World War I, which gave new political charge to the image, and it came in the same year as Raymond Duchamp-Villon's paean to "the tower and the nave." In both works —painting and writing— the modern view of Notre-Dame that Viollet-le-Duc had first promoted in his nineteenth-century theory of the Gothic was realized. Perhaps not in a way that the architect would have anticipated, Gothic architecture had nevertheless undergirded the development of modernism, and Notre-Dame had played a not inconsequential role in that phenomenon.

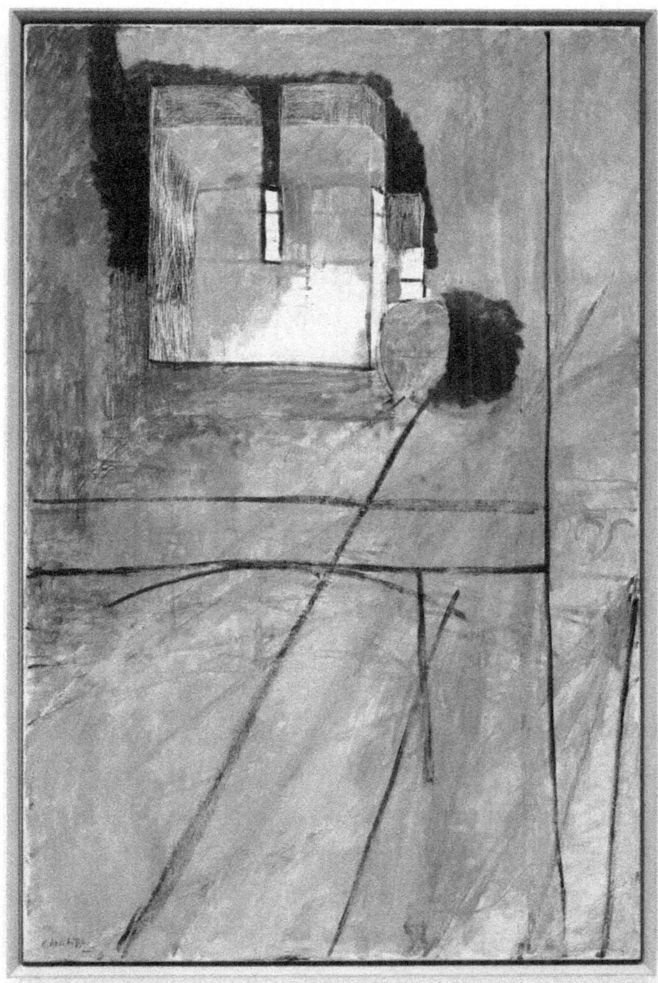

14. Henri Matisse, *View of Notre Dame. Paris, Quai Saint-Michel, Spring 1914.*

At the same time, French restoration methods, especially those employed by Viollet-le-Duc at Notre-Dame and elsewhere, were increasingly criticized, sometimes harshly. For example, in the pivotal year of 1914, the collected visual works and texts focusing on medieval French architecture by the renowned sculptor Auguste Rodin (1840-1917) were published as *Les Cathédrales de France.* Ronald R. Bernier (in his contribution to Glaser, ed., *The Idea of the Gothic Cathedral*, 2018) takes Rodin to be making an "outright attack on Viollet-le-Duc and his methods," when the sculptor says that "The true enemies of architecture and sculpture are the bad architects and sculptors, the great, fashionable surgeons who claim to 'remake', artificially, the limbs that the patient has lost." This is an apt metaphor for the transformation Viollet-le-Duc had brought about at Notre-Dame where the spire was just one of the lost appendages that the architect replaced. His approach —restoring historic buildings to their imagined completeness—made Notre-Dame into a powerful and lasting image of the French nation, however much Viollet-le-Duc would be criticized for it until a reappraisal of his contribution coalesced around the time of the centennial of his death in 1979. Whatever its shortcomings, the restoration of Notre-Dame that concluded just before the end of the Second Empire produced a monument to Gothic architecture that was incredibly flexible. It could be seen as republican, anarchist, Christian, royal, or even modernist. As the responses to the fire of April 15, 2019 demonstrated, if Viollet-le-Duc and his collaborators accomplished nothing else, they indisputably created an image of the medieval period to last the ages.

Postscript

By the fall of 2019 Notre-Dame had lost its roof and spire to fire, and the stained glass windows had been removed from the upper walls of the choir and nave for preservation. The building looked like a hollow shell and recalled nothing so much as images of Reims Cathedral at the end of World War I. Clearly, the assessment of the damage to Notre-Dame from the fire will be a long and painstaking process. The actual restoration will then add to our wait before we can enter the cathedral once again and reflect on this most recent chapter in the building's long story of construction, destruction, and reconstruction. When it is rebuilt, that restoration will reflect the twenty-first century's conception of the Gothic, just as every other previous intervention in the building bore the stamp of its own time.

In the wake of the fire, reports Hervé Grandsart in a special issue of *Connaissance des Arts* from fall 2019, the "strange idea" of an international competition to design a new spire for Notre-Dame surfaced in the press. Projects for a contemporary roof, to replace the burned wood structure, also proliferated, some of them employing glass and steel. However serious these proposals were (or were not), they did reprise debates from the nineteenth and twentieth centuries when architects and administrators had considered using concrete and iron in place of wood when cathedral roofs were repaired or rebuilt (as at Reims after World War I). Subsequent to the outpouring of contemporary projects for the new roof and spire in Paris, Philippe Villeneuve, the architect for the historic monuments agency responsible for Notre-Dame, expressed the desire that the spire be returned to its appearance before the fire, that is, the one Viollet-le-Duc had given it. As for the cathedral as a whole, Grandsart hoped that the restoration would put Notre-Dame back to what it was: "as much a tourist destination as a living cathedral apt to inspire us all over again through its appearance handed down from the nineteenth century." What's noteworthy in this statement is Grandsart's assertion that the "original" building to be resurrected is not the medieval structure, but rather the nineteenth-century cathedral brought to us by its famed restorers Viollet-le-Duc and Lassus.

Given the massive expenditure of funds the restoration will require, we inevitably will return to the question that the reporter posed to me just after the fire in April, 2019: Why should Notre-Dame, or any building, be preserved and restored? Having here summarized the cathedral's history, several answers come to mind, the most important one being that the building is a living, changing record of the past. Given that it isn't fixed but rather in a constant state of evolving, it may not always be the most reliable historic document, but as a monument at the heart of Paris, as a soaring, light-filled and undeniably impressive space, it is a very compelling one.

As we have seen, the Cathedral of Notre-Dame de Paris and its site evidence cultural, religious, political, and economic life over a span of more than one thousand years. People are touched by the histories the cathedral represents, even when those stories are of violence, intolerance, and rage. And viewers can be moved by the building emotionally, spiritually, and artistically. In any event, I believe, they are stirred by it as proof of *humanity*. We can't know very much about the lives of the people who actually constructed Notre-Dame —we don't even know the names of most of the architects who designed it. But we do know that everyone who touched the cathedral in some way expressed what it means to be human —to labor with skill or brute strength, to aspire to build something beautiful and lasting, to express one's ego, to experience abjection, and more. We live in a world that every day delivers fresh evidence of people's ability to behave inhumanely towards one another, and many aspects of our lives feel dehumanizing. So, is it not worthwhile to preserve a landmark of French history, of the Christian faith, of daring architecture and the other arts, and finally —and most importantly— a symbol of humanity?

Further reading

Amic, Sylvain and Ségolène Le Men, eds. *Cathédrales, 1789-1914, Un Mythe Moderne*. Exh. Cat. Paris: Somogy and Rouen: Musées de Rouen, 2014.

Aubert, Marcel. *Notre-Dame de Paris: Sa Place dans l'Histoire de l'Architecture du XIIe au XIVe Siècle.* [Paris]: Librarie Renouard, 1920.

Bercé, Françoise. *Viollet-le-Duc*. Paris: Éditions du Patrimoine, Centre des Monuments Nationaux, 2014.

Beurdeley, Michel. "Le Vandalisme Révolutionnaire." In *Patrimoine Parisien, 1789-1799. Destructions, Créations, Mutilations*. Ed., Alfred Fierro. Paris: Délégation à l'Action Artistique de la Ville de Paris and Bibliothèque Historique de la Ville de Paris, 1989.

Bressani, Martin. *Architecture and the Historical Imagination, Eugène-Emmanuel Viollet-le-Duc, 1814-1879*. New York: Ashgate, 2014.

Davis, Michael T. "Splendor and Peril: The Cathedral of Paris, 1290-1350. *Art Bulletin* Vol. 80, no. 1 (March 1998): 34-66.

Emery, Elizabeth. *Romancing the Cathedral: Gothic Architecture in Fin-de-Siècle French Culture*. New York: SUNY Press, 2001.

Erlande-Brandenburg, Alain. *Notre-Dame de Paris.* John Goodman, trans. New York: Harry N. Abrams, 1998.

Erlande-Brandenburg, Alain. "La Restauration de Notre-Dame de Paris au xixe siècle." *Archéologia* 141 (Avril 1980): 26-31.

Erlande-Brandenburg, Alain, Jean-Michel Leniaud, François Loyer, and Christian Michel, eds. *Autour de Notre-Dame.* Paris: Action Artistique de la Ville de Paris, 2003.

Fonquernie, Bernard. "Notre-Dame de Paris: Observations Faites sur la Galerie des Rois au cours de la Campagne de Travaux, 1998-1999." *Bulletin Monumental*, tome 157, n°4 (1999): 347-354.

Frankl, Paul. *Gothic Architecture* (1962). Revised by Paul Crossley. New Haven: Yale University Press, 2000.

Glaser, Stephanie A., ed *The Idea of the Gothic Cathedral: Interdisciplinary Perspectives on the Meanings of the Medieval Edifice in the Modern Period.* Turnhout, Belgium: Brepols, 2018.

Gómez-Moreno, Carmen. *Sculpture from Notre-Dame, Paris: A Dramatic Discovery.* New York: Metropolitan Museum of Art, 1979.

Guilhermy, Ferdinand de and E.E. Viollet-le-Duc. *Description de Notre-Dame, Cathédrale de Paris*. Paris: P. Bance, 1856.

Lassus, Jean-Baptise and E.E. Viollet-le-Duc. *Projet de Restauration de Notre-Dame de Paris.Rapport Addresseé à M. le Ministre de la Justice et des Cultes, Annexé au Projet de Restauration, Remis le 31 Janvier 1843*. Paris: Imprimerie de Mme. De Lacombe, 1843.

Leniaud, Jean-Michel. *Jean-Baptiste Lassus [1807-1857] ou Le Temps Retrouvé des Cathédrales*. Genève: Droz and Paris: Arts et Métiers Graphiques, 1980.

Murphy, Kevin D. *Memory and Modernity: Viollet-le-Duc at Vézelay*. University Park: Penn State Press, 2000.

Murray, Stephen. "Notre-Dame of Paris and the Anticipation of the Gothic." *Art Bulletin* 80 (June 1998): 229-53.

Poisson, Georges and Olivier Poisson. *Eugène Viollet-le-Duc, 1814-1879*. Paris: A. & J. Picard, 2014.

Sandron, Dany, Jean-Pierre Cartier, Gérard Pelletier et al. *La Grâce d'une Cathédrale, Notre-Dame de Paris*. Strasbourg: Éditions du Quotidien/ La Nuée Bleue, 2012-19.

Sandron, Dany and Andrew J. Tallon. *Notre-Dame de Paris: Neuf Siècles d'Histoire*. Paris: Parigramme, 2013.

Sankovitch, Anne-Marie. "Structure/Ornament and the Modern Figuration of Architecture." *Art Bulletin* Vol. 80 (Dec. 1998): 687-717.

Tallon, Andrew J. "Rethinking Medieval Structure." In *New Approaches to Medieval Architecture*, ed. Robert Bork, William Clark and Abby McGehee. Farnham: Ashgate, 2011.

Viollet-le-Duc, Eugène-Emmanuel. *The Foundations of Architecture. Selections from the Dictionnaire Raisonné*. Kenneth Whitehead, trans. New York: George Braziller, 1990.

Viollet-le-Duc, Eugène-Emmanuel. "La Flèche de Notre-Dame." *Gazette des Beaux-Arts* 1 (April 1860): 35-39.

Von Simson, Otto. *The Gothic Cathedral: Origins of Gothic Architecture and the Medieval Concept of Order*. New York: Pantheon Books, 1956.

Westgate, Deirdre and Charanne Clarke. "Notre-Dame de Paris: The Apostles on the Spire Rediscovered." *Burlington Magazine* 149, No. 1253, Painting and Sculpture in France (Aug. 2007): 537-545.

A Quick Immersion series

1 **De-Extinctions,** Carles Lalueza-Fox

2 **Populisms,** Carlos de la Torre

3 **Happiness,** Amitava Krishna Dutt and Benjamin Radcliff

4 **The Science of Cooking,** Claudi Mans

5 **Aristotle,** C.D.C. Reeve

6 **Jewish Culture,** Jess Olson

7 **Fascism,** Roger Griffin

8 **Nonviolence,** Andrew Fiala

9 **The French Revolution,** Jay Smith

10 **Jazz,** Joel Dinerstein

11 **The Cathedral of Notre-Dame of Paris,** Kevin D. Murphy

www.ingramcontent.com/pod-product-compliance
Lightning Source LLC
La Vergne TN
LVHW010059110826
845155LV00028B/406

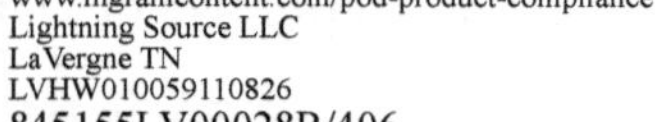